M000167460

IF ONLY I'D KNOWN!

How to Outsmart Narcissists, Set Guilt-Free Boundaries, and Create Unshakeable Self-Worth

CHELSEY BROOKE COLE,

LPC-MHSP, CPTT, RPT

PRAISE FOR *IF ONLY I'D KNOWN!*

"Chelsey is able to describe exactly what I went through and what others have endured in a concise way. It is so important for mental health professionals to shine a light on this insidious form of domestic violence so that our clients, readers, and followers can get the validation and support that they so desperately need. She is an advocate for trauma survivors and her writing will help so many people to become empowered and heal."
—Vanessa Reiser, LCSW, Narcissistic/Cult Abuse Expert

"Chelsey Cole's book on narcissistic abuse is an exceptional and empathetic guide, offering deep insights and compassion for those on a journey of understanding and healing. With a profound understanding of the subject matter and personal experiences to draw from, Cole's perspective is both enlightening and empowering. The author effortlessly breaks down complex concepts, making them accessible and relatable to survivors who are grappling with the aftermath of narcissistic abuse. For anyone in search of clarity, healing, and a renewed sense of hope, this book is an absolute must-read." *—Tracy Malone, Author, Founder of NarcissistAbuseSupport.com, International Coach, and Speaker*

"I've always considered myself to be a bold, confident, high achiever. But my experience with narcissistic abuse in a personal relationship shook me to my core. It crushed my spirit and broke my heart. Narcissistic abuse affected every aspect of my inner life, and I felt stuck. Chelsey's insights were such a gift to me, offering clarity, affirmation, and mindsets for recovery and healing. As I read her words, I often felt like she was reading my mind and speaking directly to the abuse I had gone through. I'm grateful to Chelsey and will certainly be sharing this book with others. Highly recommended!" *—Brett Culp, Acclaimed Documentary Filmmaker & Speaker*

"People dealing with this kind of insidious abuse often feel completely alone. Chelsey explains what's happening and why, adding a deep dose of comfort. Thanks for an excellent resource, and we will surely be recommending this book to our community!"—Lisa Johnson and Chris Barry, High-Conflict Divorce Coaches and Authors of Been There Got Out

"If you're a quiet overthinker with a kind heart who struggles to set healthy boundaries, then you can be taken advantage of by a narcissist. Your caring heart and willingness to see the good in people are gifts that need protection. To protect yourself from toxic people, you need to do two things: educate yourself on narcissists, and set authentic, sustainable boundaries. And that's exactly what Chelsey teaches you to do. Any introvert who's experienced narcissistic abuse or toxic relationships needs to read this book." –Matthew Pollard, Bestselling Author of The Introvert's Edge series

"Chelsey is able to put into words what every narcissistic abuse survivor feels. She gives voice to those who don't know how to say what they've been through. She is a true advocate for trauma survivors of all kinds, including those harmed by romantic partners, parents, siblings, and friends." –Tracy Fields, BSW, MSW, Therapist and Speaker

"This book is a survivor manual for narcissistic abuse survivors. Chelsey clearly and relatably explains not only how to understand narcissists, but also how to heal from manipulative and abusive relationships. This book is so much more than an explanation of narcissistic behaviors—it's a lifeboat that will take you to a place of healing, empowerment, and total transformation." –Steve Friedman, Award-Winning Author of The Corporate Introvert: How to Lead and Thrive with Confidence

"Early in my career—when working as an administrative assistant in Hollywood—I had the misfortune of reporting to one horrible boss after another. With only a few exceptions, most of these managers were

tyrannical, arrogant, egomaniacal, abusive bullies who inflated their own egos and status by manipulating, lying to, gaslighting, belittling, intimidating, and threatening those around and beneath them. And the toxic cultures of many of these entertainment industry companies appeared to deem these abhorrent behaviors to be totally acceptable. In fact, the trauma of these early career work experiences (which I've since labeled as "PTBD" or "Post-Traumatic Boss Disorder" as the memories and some of the pain still lingers) is what eventually led to my becoming an executive coach and leadership professor. What I did not truly realize—until reading Chelsey Brooke Cole's insightful and inspirational new book—is that these awful bosses were all narcissists. As the title of this wonderful piece of work states, "If Only I'd Known" that how I was being treated was entirely unacceptable, emotionally unhealthy, not my fault, and completely not normal, I might have been better able to identify, understand, and navigate some of these difficult and painful situations, and more quickly and successfully regain my self-worth and reclaim my power. This book is a must-read for anyone who is dealing with a narcissist in either their personal or professional life, as it will not only help you to recognize, define, and validate your experience, but—with the help of Chelsey's understanding, empathetic, and compassionate style—will provide you with a variety of ways to deal with your situation and take greater ownership of your life." –Todd Cherches, CEO of BigBlueGumball and Author of VisuaLeadership: Leveraging the Power of Visual Thinking in Leadership and in Life

IF ONLY I'D KNOWN!

How to Outsmart Narcissists, Set Guilt-Free Boundaries, and Create Unshakeable Self-Worth

Copyright © 2023 Chelsey Brooke Cole, LPC-MHSP, CPTT, RPT

All rights reserved. No part of this book may be reproduced or used in any manner without the prior written permission of the copyright owner, except for the use of brief quotations in a book review.

The information in this book was correct at the time of publication, but the author does not assume any liability for loss or damage caused by errors or omissions. To maintain the anonymity of the individuals involved, some details or identifying information has been changed.

The content of this book is for informational purposes only and is not intended to diagnose, treat, cure, or prevent any condition or disease. You understand that this book is not intended as a substitute for consultation with a licensed practitioner. Please consult with your own physician or healthcare specialist regarding the suggestions and recommendations made in this book. The use of this book implies your acceptance of this disclaimer.

Library of Congress Control Number: 2023909472

Paperback ISBN 979-8-9884097-0-0

Hardcover ISBN 979-8-9884097-1-7

Ebook ISBN 979-8-9884097-2-4

Audiobook ISBN 979-8-9884097-3-1

Editor: George Verongos

Cover design: Matt Hall and George Verongos

Author photograph: Cassie Adkins

Book cover artist: Stacey Lee

1st edition, August 2023

Printed in the United States of America

10 9 8 7 6 5 4 3 2 1

IF ONLY I'D KNOWN!

How to Outsmart Narcissists,
Set Guilt-Free Boundaries, and
Create Unshakeable Self-Worth

CHELSEY BROOKE COLE,
LPC-MHSP, CPTT, RPT

Download
the first
chapter for
FREE!

As a thank you for buying my
book, I'd like to give you the
e-book first chapter for free!

To download go to:

www.chelseybrookecole.com/firstchapterfree

Quiz
TIME

Ever wondered if your parent or partner is a narcissist?

Have questions on what being narcissistically abused feels like?

Have concerns that you're being gaslighted?

Take these 2-minute quizzes to gain clarity now!

www.chelseybrookecole.com/quizzes

CONTENTS

PART TWO
FINDING YOURSELF

PART THREE
HEALING YOUR PAST, PRESENT, AND
FUTURE

PREFACE

"I can't believe I'm in this situation again." "Why do I keep doing this to myself?" "I'll never be good enough." These thoughts frantically raced through my mind as I tried to make sense of my life and my choices. This wasn't the first time I had been betrayed, lied to, and hurt, which made my self-blame even louder. I cried in my car and internally screamed, *"I should've known better ... honestly, I'm a therapist!"*

But these silent criticisms didn't make me feel any better. In fact, they only made me feel worse. First, because self-blame is completely unproductive. And second, because the person I was with at the time was more than willing to let me take the blame for everything. Which meant anytime I took personal responsibility, they used it as "proof" that I was the one causing the problems all along.

They told me that if I were more patient, they wouldn't be so defensive; that if I were more affectionate, they wouldn't have to wander; that if I weren't so difficult, they wouldn't have to rage at me.

And for years, I accepted these manipulations as truths. I bought into the idea that if I could be perfect, I could be loved. And based on my childhood, this felt familiar ... expected ... normal. As if perpetually trying to earn someone's love, attention, and loyalty was what everyone was doing.

I made a lot of excuses for people back then. I mean *a lot*. I equated giving second chances with loving someone. I confused tolerating abuse with being loyal. I mistook people-pleasing for being empathetic. I allowed all my genuinely good qualities to be twisted and used against me.

Back then, I didn't have a name for what I was experiencing. I didn't know that some people understood what you needed, they just didn't care. I didn't accept that some people genuinely don't want to be better. I didn't realize that some people only care about you to the extent that they can use you. And that when they're done with you, they will throw you out of their life like they throw out the garbage.

Being treated like you're disposable hurts. But I had to learn that others' poor treatment of me didn't have to turn into my own poor treatment of myself. I had to learn not to allow others to tell me who I should be. I had to learn to trust my intuition even when I didn't have all the answers. I had to learn to listen to my own voice because I was the one who had to live with the consequences.

Years of feeling broken led me to eventually break. But from that broken place, I put the pieces back together in a way that felt genuine, authentic, and secure. I didn't build my new sense of self on what others thought of me. I didn't look to others to define me. I realized that the instruction manual for building me couldn't be found outside of me. So, I built a new me. And she's stronger than she ever was before.

This book was created out of my pain, which turned into my purpose. After years of experiencing narcissistic abuse, healing from it, and helping so many others do the same, I wanted to create a tangible roadmap for anyone who is dealing with or has dealt with the effects of narcissistic abuse.

My hope is that you take this book's contents and make it your own. That you take what resonates and leave the rest. That you learn to appreciate your strengths, have compassion for your vulnerabilities, and build your sense of self on solid ground.

In preparation for this book, I collected stories from over four hundred narcissistic abuse survivors and sourced information from peer-reviewed articles, books, online forums, case studies, and my own community of over thirty thousand narcissistic abuse survivors.

As a licensed psychotherapist and certified partner trauma therapist, I've spent thousands of clinical hours helping people understand and heal from narcissistic abuse and relationship trauma. All these resources and experiences were reviewed, written, and revised to create a comprehensive and therapeutically sound guide for your healing journey.

I hope you find this book validating, empowering, and refreshing to your heart. You deserve to feel seen, understood, cared for, and loved. I pray these pages help you feel those things and positively impact the way you see yourself, others, and the world forever.

Warmly,

Chelsey

PART ONE

THE INNER WORKINGS OF A NARCISSIST

CHAPTER ONE

Why You're Here

"I constantly ask myself: How did I end up with someone like him? How did I not see?"
—Beth

If you're reading this, there's a good chance you've been personally impacted by at least one narcissist in your life. Maybe the narcissist was your critical parent, unfaithful partner, attention-grabbing sibling, or backstabbing friend. Maybe the narcissist was your cold and emotionally distant mother, your triangulating co-worker, your unrelenting boss, or your exceptionally grandiose father. And chances are, no matter who the narcissist was (or is) in your life, you felt the sting and fear of never being good enough.

Feeling not enough is the mantra for narcissistic relationships. They leave you feeling broken, depressed, anxious, hypervigilant, foggy, stuck, and bruised to your soul. They extract the goodness from your heart, the light out of your world, and the belief in anything good. They make you question yourself, doubt your reality, second-guess every decision, and ruminate over every interaction and conversation. They make you lose ... you.

And feeling as if your identity, your very core, has been slowly and silently smashed into a thousand pieces is heartbreaking, gut-wrenching, and devastating. You wonder…

"How did I get here?"

"What am I supposed to do now?"

"Who am I?"

"Where do I start?"

"Will I ever feel like 'me' again?"

"What do I even want or need?"

If you can relate, let me reassure you: these questions are completely normal! And as hopeless, confused, regretful, and scared as you might be, please hear me when I say … there *is* a way out. A way to *get back to being you*. A way to find yourself, maybe even for the *very first time*.

Whatever your story, let me take a moment to welcome you to this book. You're not here by accident. You kept asking, seeking, and knocking until you came to this place. You were meant to be here, in this moment, reading this book right now. I believe that when we're ready, what we're looking for finds us. And I'm so glad we found each other.

On this road to healing, we have several important sites to see. This book is divided into three parts. The first part focuses on helping you gain a clear picture of what a narcissist looks like in all its forms (we'll cover six types of narcissists) and understand the narcissistic relationship. The second part is about helping you reflect on how you got here (including demystifying the ever-elusive trauma bond) and the life experiences that shaped your beliefs about yourself, others, and the world.

The third part provides must-have insights and practical strategies for lasting growth. If you felt like you had a strong sense of self *before* the narcissistic relationship but are struggling to rediscover yourself again, you'll find the strategies in this section refreshing and inspiring. And if you feel like you've always struggled to know yourself or that you get lost in helping others or people-pleasing, you'll resonate with the sensitive and empowering strategies found in this section.

Your healing journey includes:

PART ONE: THE INNER WORKINGS OF A NARCISSIST

Chapter 1 – Why You're Here

Chapter 2 – Narcissist: From Buzzword to Betrayer

Chapter 3 – The Look and Feel of Narcissists: Recognizing Six Different Types

Chapter 4 – The Narcissistic Cycle of Abuse: Idealize, Devalue, Discard, Hoover

Chapter 5 – Narcissistic Love Bombing: How Different Types Do It

Chapter 6 – Narcissistic Abuse: Uncovering the Layers of Deception and Chaos

PART TWO: FINDING YOURSELF

Chapter 7 – Am I Being Abused? How Your Body Warns You of Toxic Relationships

Although the focus of this book is primarily on helping you heal from intimate relationships with narcissists, the explanations and strategies apply to any narcissistic relationship (i.e., friendship, work relationship, family relationship, etc.). Throughout this book, you'll find stories from narcissistic abuse survivors who share their experiences with narcissistic parents, siblings, partners, bosses, etc.

This book also provides several real-world examples so you can get a clear picture of what each type of narcissist looks and feels like. Whether you were completely blindsided by your toxic relationship, have experienced several narcissistic relationships, or just want to protect yourself from ever getting into these relationships, this book is for you.

Narcissistic relationships steal your time and peace of mind and leave you feeling like a shell of a person. Narcissists have stolen enough. Stop putting your hope in them. It's your turn to grieve, grow, and heal. Narcissists might've stolen your past, and they might even be trying to steal your present. Don't let them steal your future too. That belongs to **you**! Let's get started building it.

CHAPTER TWO

Narcissist: From Buzzword to Betrayer

"I'm so extremely betrayed. And that is a very difficult thing I have to accept and start to heal from. I was shattered in a million pieces."
—Anonymous

"Something isn't right here."

Throughout my life, I had this thought about my relationships countless times. I could never put my finger on exactly what the problem was, even though the same issues kept coming up. The same arguments, the same hurt and confusion, and the same self-doubts and insecurities.

I wondered repeatedly, *"What's wrong with me?" "Am I being too sensitive?" "Maybe I expect too much," "Will I ever get this right?"* without any real clarity or understanding.

We're told, "Relationships are hard work," so, I tried harder. We're told, "It's a communication issue," so, I tried every communication strategy. We're told, "They just need time to mature," or "He loves you; he just doesn't know how to show it sometimes," so, I married him and gave him time, patience, and love.

But conventional advice never made my relationships better, only worse. Which meant for most of my life, I thought I was the problem. I thought that if I could be good enough, kind enough, giving enough, loyal enough … then I could earn love.

And I tried, and tried, and tried … for years. As a child, I tried to be perfect, so I could be loved. As a teenager, I made excuses for inexcusable behaviors because I thought they would change. As an adult, I ignored my gut when it screamed at me to walk away from toxic partners.

And then, one day, something inside of me broke. I realized that I would end up sacrificing my whole life for someone if I didn't stop looking at potential instead of reality. Perhaps for the first time in my life, I stopped, breathed, and listened to my gut. I looked at my current relationship and saw things as they were, not as I hoped they could be. I accepted that how things *had been* was how they would always be.

The inconsistencies, lies, and manipulations wouldn't stop. The promises that were made and broken wouldn't stop. The blame-shifting, rage, and passive-aggressiveness wouldn't stop. The criticisms, comparisons, and callousness wouldn't stop.

Time slowed down, hope drained from my heart, and the reality of the situation set in. I had given everything, and it still wasn't enough. And despite years of self-reflection, I had overlooked this one massive truth: *it wasn't about me.* There was nothing I could do to make things better because you can't fix problems you're not causing. And at that moment, I was both heartbroken and free.

My relationship problems weren't about me, and yours *aren't about you.* You're not crazy. You're not worthless. You're not unlovable.

You've been hurt, betrayed, and rejected. You've been lied to, manipulated, and cut to the heart. You might feel confused, overwhelmed, hurt, anxious, foggy, and stuck. You might feel like you don't even know who you are anymore. You might feel in this moment that you're alone. That no one gets what you're going through. And that's a very understandable feeling.

Thoughts like, *"Why is this happening?" "What am I doing wrong?" "Am I going crazy?"* are common when you're trying to make sense of what you're experiencing. And that's why understanding narcissism and narcissistic abuse is the best place to start your healing because you can't heal from what you don't understand.

So, what does it mean to be a narcissist? What behaviors and patterns should you be looking for? Let's break down this elusive term once and for all.

WHAT IS A NARCISSIST?

"He was so outgoing, full of energy, and gave me so much attention and what seemed like love and adoration which I lacked my whole life, so it felt so good to me to be recognized."
—Yvonne, speaking of narcissistic ex-husband

"We got along as young children, and I just went along with her bossiness because I was the younger sister. As I got older, I started wanting my own space ... Most of the time when a fight broke out, I had to be the mediator. For years I watched my sister throw fits when she didn't get what she wanted ... I always knew something was wrong with her but never knew what it was."
—Anonymous, speaking of narcissistic sister

"I did not know my parents were narcissists as a child, but I knew from a very young age that there was something about them I did not trust."
—Anonymous, speaking of narcissistic parents

Narcissist—you've heard the term thrown around to describe difficult in-laws, selfish friends, and cheating partners. But what does this word really mean? And what makes it worth devoting a whole book to?

You might be surprised to learn that millions of people just like you are experiencing the impacts of narcissism. Yes, you read that right: *millions*. You are not alone! Lifetime prevalence rates of narcissistic personality disorder (NPD) are roughly six percent.[1]

That means in the United States, almost 20 million people meet the criteria for NPD. If those 20 million narcissists negatively impact five other people (a conservative estimate), that means *99 million* people will experience some form of narcissistic abuse in the United States alone.

Keep in mind that someone doesn't have to be diagnosed with NPD to cause damage. That's because narcissism is a personality trait that exists on a spectrum. At the low end of the spectrum, people are vain, overly concerned with appearance or status, and exhibit little to no empathy. Think of the charming, gregarious friend who's great for livening up dinner parties but has little capacity for meaningful conversations or showing empathy.

At the high end of the narcissism spectrum, people are vengeful, manipulative, sadistic[2] (i.e., gain pleasure from people's pain), malevolent[3] (i.e., malicious), and paranoid. Think of the power-obsessed CEO who's been quietly embezzling millions with no concern for those his actions will impact.

Narcissism is characterized by certain patterns,[4] including things like:

- An excessive need for admiration
- Constant validation seeking

- Self-absorption

- Feelings of superiority

- An inflated sense of self-importance

- Variable to low empathy

- Extreme sensitivity to criticism or feedback

- Emotional reactivity

- Interpersonal exploitativeness

Because narcissism is a personality trait that exhibits relatively predictable patterns of behavior over time, calling someone a "narcissist" is a descriptive term, not a diagnosis. Saying someone is "narcissistic" is like saying someone is "agreeable," "conscientious," or "extroverted."

Obviously, these descriptions can be misused if they are overgeneralized, such as when we call someone "introverted" because they decide to stay home on a Friday night. Similarly, it wouldn't be appropriate to call someone "narcissistic" because they excitedly shared about their recent promotion or reacted defensively one time in the last six months.

Keeping this in mind, and for purposes of clarity, a "narcissist" in this book is defined as someone who displays, at minimum, a pervasive pattern of grandiosity, entitlement, exploitativeness, lack of empathy, superficial relationships, and an excessive need for admiration. Let's look at each of these patterns a little more closely.

EXCESSIVE NEED FOR ADMIRATION

Everyone appreciates support, recognition, or positive feedback every now and then. But narcissists need it to get through the day. Narcissists live off people's attention, admiration, praise, and validation. Narcissists' self-esteem is largely contingent on meeting some external standard, meaning how they feel about themselves varies from moment to moment, depending on how much they're being noticed and approved of.

Narcissists seek validation and praise to support their fragile egos. Whatever is feeding the narcissist's ego is said to be giving them narcissistic supply. Essentially, supply is the narcissist's version of self-esteem. This is why they care about their reputation and not their character. How they feel about themselves is based on other people's perceptions, not on reality.

INFLATED SENSE OF SELF-IMPORTANCE

Grandiosity and entitlement are hallmark traits of narcissism. Narcissists believe they are "better than," special, or exceptionally unique and have an unrealistic sense of superiority. Grandiosity and the need to be seen as special pushes narcissists to tout their achievements, brag about their accomplishments and expect to be given special treatment.

Narcissistic grandiosity can include things like attempting to be the center of attention, constantly posting on social media to get likes, believing they're never wrong, feeling like they're better, smarter, or more deserving than anyone else, or engaging in fantasies about how important, smart, talented, or powerful they are.

Narcissists' entitlement also means they're incredibly hypocritical. They have one set of rules for themself and one set of rules for the rest of the world. When *they* have something important, relevant, exciting, or difficult to share, they expect your full attention and support, even though they don't give this in return.

EMOTIONAL FRAGILITY

Despite their often grandiose or charming exterior, narcissists are emotionally vulnerable, meaning they're hypersensitive to criticism, emotionally reactive, and experience intense feelings of inferiority and inadequacy.[5] They are impulsive and emotionally fragile.

This fragility leads narcissists to do things like become sullen or rageful after a small criticism or constructive feedback, act sad or hurt to get people's attention or sympathy, and deny any wrongdoing to avoid feelings of shame.

When narcissists display their vulnerable side, they say things like, "Why doesn't the world see how great I am?" "Why is everyone always out to get me?" or "Life's so unfair to me!" Narcissists' self-esteem is highly fragile, which is why they get stuck obsessing about why people don't treat them with more admiration, feeling sorry for themselves, believing they're always the victim, or ruminating on ways to avenge real or perceived wrongs.

LACK OF EMPATHY

Narcissists have variable to minimal empathy and hold a basic contempt for human emotions. This means they feel disgusted, irritated, or annoyed when you share your feelings, are going through a difficult time, or need support or compassion.

Narcissists view others' expressions of emotion as a sign of weakness or simply as an inconvenience. They might coldly say you're "selfish," "inconsiderate," or "pathetic" for wanting them to listen to your feelings and that you should "stop feeling sorry for yourself."

Narcissists' default is to see everything from their perspective and their perspective only. They don't think about how others feel or what they want or need.

Depending on where they fall on the narcissism spectrum, they either overlook your feelings because they're completely preoccupied with their own, or they intentionally seek to harm you to gain a sense of power and control. They also don't consider how their actions impact you, especially if they haven't received much validation or praise lately.

EXTREME SELF-ABSORPTION

Narcissists say *what* they want, *when* they want, *how* they want, and expect you to get over it quite quickly. For example, narcissists will cheat on you and expect things to go back to normal within a few weeks. They will say incredibly hurtful things in an argument, throw a "sorry" at you later, and expect your hurt feelings to subside immediately.

If you ask why the same hurtful things keep happening or for restitution to be made, they'll say you're "unforgiving," "unable to let things go," or wanting to "hold a grudge." They don't like to curb their emotions or use self-control. If it's on their mind, they want to say it without repercussions.

Narcissists' selfishness is also why you get criticized for doing things like going to work, picking up the kids from school, or engaging in a healthy hobby because none of those things are *for* the narcissist personally.

INTERPERSONAL EXPLOITATIVENESS

Narcissists view relationships in a very transactional way. They don't want your love. They want your admiration. Narcissists have a need to be adored, and *you* have the supply. They want you to fill up their bottomless cup with attention, praise, desire, compliments, and unrelenting affection.

Whereas healthy people create relationships based on respect, cooperation, mutuality, and kindness, narcissists build their relationships on control, manipulation, and deceit. They present a false self to get you into the relationship, slowly devalue you to gain control of your emotions and perceptions, then discard you through lying, cheating, silent treatments, gaslighting, or leaving the relationship.

NARCISSISTIC DEFENSES

Defense mechanisms are subconscious or automatic reactions that attempt to regulate internal conflicts.[6] And narcissists ... have a lot of internal conflicts. Because they hold an idealized version of themselves, they become upset when the outside world doesn't affirm their "greatness."

Instead of reflecting on this disparity and attempting to build a healthy (not inflated) sense of self-worth, they engage in defense mechanisms to maintain their entitled and grandiose image.

For example, let's say a grandiose narcissist holds himself to be the most valuable employee in the company—but someone else gets the promotion he believes he deserves. At this point, the narcissist will experience a mix of shame, injustice, and outrage. These highly unsettling and uncomfortable emotions typically show up as defenses, like denial, rage, contempt, blame-shifting, and projection.

DENIAL

For narcissists, if they don't admit it, they don't have to deal with it. Whether you want to confirm a previously agreed-upon time for dinner, confront an inconsistency, address a reoccurring issue, or revisit an old conversation, narcissists' denial makes all this impossible.

They deny things they said or did, even within the last twenty-four hours. They deny ever having a conversation about a particular topic, hearing an important detail you shared (even though they acknowledged you at the time), or being somewhere with someone, even if you physically saw it with your own eyes.

To make matters worse, they will deny truths even when you have proof or evidence. They lie even when they're caught, when it doesn't make sense, and when *not* lying would be better for them. A "normal" liar will admit to the lie when they're caught, even if they still defend their choices. Narcissists lie regardless of the evidence.

RAGE

Rage takes on a whole new meaning when you witness it from a narcissist. Let's say you caught them in a lie, have proof of the affair, or try having a conversation with them about their reckless behaviors. In these instances, the narcissist is confronted with reality and is no longer able to hide behind their illusion. The curtain has dropped, and *they know you know* who they really are.

Instead of self-reflecting, narcissists rage by calling you "crazy," "jealous," "controlling," or "too sensitive." Narcissistic rage is out of proportion to the situation and seems immature, unreasonable, and unprovoked. They become incredibly passive-aggressive, calling you names, insulting your efforts, or ignoring your attempts to compromise.

The intensity of this rage can be disturbing, unnerving, and frightening. These fits of rage make it impossible to resolve conflict or come to respectful resolutions.

Not only does narcissistic rage protect the narcissist from facing the reality of their choices, but it also conditions you to *walk on eggshells* or not bring up certain topics. Because you begin to feel that the narcissist is erratic, unstable, or unpredictable, you become trained to act in ways that support the narcissist's ego, giving them praise, admiration, and attention so as not to "set them off."

This, of course, is a slippery slope that can lead to enabling and justifying abusive behaviors.

CONTEMPT

To best understand how and why narcissists experience so much contempt, you need to remember narcissists' core issues: they're pathologically insecure, exceedingly entitled, and need to be seen as "better than" to maintain their grandiose idea of themselves. And most narcissists (except for perhaps the malignant narcissist) really don't like themselves. Essentially, they have a lot of self-contempt.

However, narcissists don't self-reflect; they project. So instead of identifying and addressing their self-loathing, they project their *self*-disdain and *self*-contempt onto everyone else and everything they know they should be … but aren't. They hold contempt for:

- Anything good, like kindness, respect, or compassion.

- Anything they don't have, like fancy cars, a big house, or nice clothes.

- Anyone who succeeds more than them, like their boss, wealthy brother, or well-respected neighbor.

When narcissists feel contemptuous, they feel better than. It's a way to look down on someone or something as if it's beneath them. They don't have to acknowledge their real feelings of sadness, jealousy, or self-loathing if they act disgusted with and superior to the good and admirable traits, qualities, or successes of those around them.

This helps them regulate their emotions and maintain their false sense of self as they convince themselves that others' achievements, emotions, or needs are weak, pathetic, and ridiculous.

BLAME-SHIFTING

Blame-shifting is denial's more sophisticated cousin. When narcissists engage in the defense mechanism of blame-shifting, they're both denying their part in the matter and targeting *you* as the one who's guilty. This serves many purposes.

It *distracts* from the real issue, attempts to *distort* your reality, and pushes you to *defend* your truth. If narcissists can successfully distract you from the initial issue, they don't have to be held accountable for their actions or explain themselves.

This distraction process can distort your reality of what's happened because, during emotional conversations, it's easy to get confused and thrown off balance if someone immediately brings up another issue before addressing the first one.

And if you're distracted, and the reality of the situation gets distorted, you're likely to start defending, justifying, explaining, or personalizing the narcissist's statements. These tactics shield the narcissist from being confronted with the consequences of their actions or feeling the gravity of their choices.

PROJECTION

Projection is a defense mechanism that relates to the narcissist's lack of ability or willingness to engage in productive self-reflection. To put it simply, projection is like looking into a mirror. You don't see people as *they* are; you see people as *you* are.

People act like reflections, showing *you* who *you* are. Since narcissists are insecure, manipulative, and vengeful, they believe others are as well. To quote Anaïs Nin, "We don't see the world as it is – we see it as **we** are."

For example, when narcissists cheat, it's very common for them to consistently accuse *you* of being unfaithful. When narcissists lie, they act convinced that *you* are the one who's bending the truth. This hypocrisy adds to the confusion and crazy making you already feel by being in a relationship with a narcissist.

To gain more clarity, think of it like this: projections are confessions. Whatever narcissists accuse *you* of feeling or doing is likely how *they* feel or what *they* are doing. However, don't expect to share this insight with a narcissist and have them admit to the truth.

Narcissists lack insight into why they do what they do, which is why you won't get them to acknowledge this kind of thing. Fortunately for us, awareness is power! Even if the narcissist never gets it … *you can.* And insight into what's happening is your bridge to sanity and empowerment.

Side note: it's also possible to project your positive traits, like empathy, kindness, and good intentions onto someone else. Survivors often do this, believing that the narcissist "didn't real mean it" or "doesn't understand" how hurtful something is because they can't believe someone would be so knowingly cruel. Don't confuse your good intentions for theirs. Just because you wouldn't say, do, or think those harmful things doesn't mean someone else wouldn't. Don't give narcissists more credit than they've shown you they deserve.

WRAPPING UP NARCISSISTIC PATTERNS

If you'd like to see these patterns in checklist form to determine if you're dealing with a narcissist, download my free narcissist checklist at https://www.chelseybrookecole.com/checklist or scan the QR code.

While all narcissists share similar patterns, not all narcissists have the same presentation, which is why understanding the different narcissistic types is essential. In chapter three, we'll explore the look and feel of six narcissistic types so you can recognize a narcissist regardless of their outward presence or demeanor.

CHAPTER THREE

The Look and Feel of Narcissists: Recognizing Six Different Types

"I had to ask, 'Is this abuse?' I really wasn't sure. He sent me bunches of flowers to the house with gushing cards 'to my beautiful, caring wife' etc. By that point I had realized that his words had not matched his actions for years and saw them for what they were. False promises. Anything to get me back in. I wasn't going to fall for his lies again."
—Miss B

Narcissistic types can *look* and *feel* different to the point at which you might not even recognize someone as *being* a narcissist if they don't match what you *expect* a narcissist to look like. This is why it's so important to be aware of different types, including what they look like and how you feel when you encounter them.

Typically, narcissists have a flavor to them, where one type fits them best. However, it's possible for narcissists to be a mix of these types. For example, you might encounter a malignant communal narcissist (like a cult leader) or a self-righteous grandiose narcissist (like a secretly abusive, outwardly moralistic preacher). Regardless of the type, they're all built on the same core issues: pathological insecurity, antagonistic defense mechanisms, low empathy, entitlement, grandiose sense of self, and incessant validation-seeking behaviors.

GRANDIOSE NARCISSISTS

Grandiose narcissists[1] are what most people think of when they hear the term narcissist. They tend to be charming, charismatic, extroverted, talkative, social, and outwardly confident. They come across as arrogant, entitled, and superior.

They tend to have lots of friends (or at least acquaintances) and seem to be successful, put together, and productive since this is the image they want to portray to the world. Here are a few examples of what grandiose narcissists look like:

- The "know it all" co-worker who steals everyone's ideas and tries to look like the go-to guy, even though he does more talking than working.

- The incredibly charming boss who throws the most lavish holiday parties, where he expects to be praised and admired; however, during the rest of the year, he doesn't have time to be bothered with your requests.

- Your partner who needs to be the center of attention and seems to have minimal interest in things that aren't about him/her.

RECOGNIZING GRANDIOSE NARCISSISTS BASED ON HOW YOU FEEL

"On the first date, he said that he had not wanted to marry again, but when he met me, it got him to reconsider. He seemed to be a

very good man who had been burned by two ex-wives who were after his money/lifestyle. He was fun to be with. In the beginning, he was very affectionate and affirmative. He is very charming. He gave me a lot of thoughtful gifts, like sending me flowers and buying expensive coffee that I liked. Also, he asked me some deeply personal questions in the beginning, and I trusted him. I shared a lot of painful experiences, and he was so compassionate. When I had to go to the ER, he showed up and said, 'Rayetta, you don't have to do this stuff alone anymore. Now you have a partner.' It sealed the deal."
–Rayetta

Grandiose narcissists pull people in through charm and charisma. People describe grandiose narcissists as having a seductive or alluring presence, almost like there's some special energy about them that you can't quite put into words. You might feel captivated by them, enamored with their charm, or attracted to (in a romantic or platonic way) their confidence.

On the other hand, if you're a sensitive person who prefers quieter or less showy personalities, you might feel like they're too much or be completely turned off by their larger-than-life presentation.

If you're the target (i.e., main source of narcissistic supply) of a grandiose narcissist, you initially feel important, seen, understood, admired, and desired. You feel lucky or special to be with them since they give off the impression that *everyone* wants them, but they chose you.

Of course, this specialness wears off once you've been in the relationship for a while since narcissists get bored quite easily and start searching for new narcissistic supply.

VULNERABLE NARCISSISTS

Vulnerable narcissists[2] (also called victimized or covert narcissists) are quiet, reserved, introverted, and not as socially adept as grandiose narcissists. At gatherings or social events, they appear withdrawn, sullen, or anxious. They have an unassuming, meek, and at times, kind demeanor. They display contemptuous social anxiety, in which they subtly or passive-aggressively criticize other guests for being too talkative, pompous, or gaudy.

Vulnerable narcissists typically have one of two presentations, depending on what serves them best at the time. The first presentation is very sullen, depressed, and victimized. They come across as jaded or mistreated and talk about past situations in which they portray themselves as having been taken advantage of, betrayed, used, or even abused.

The second presentation is one of being the *nice guy* or *sweet girl*. Vulnerable narcissists use these covers to create a lot of chaos, drama, or conflict behind the scenes since no one thinks that someone so *nice* would ever do something cruel. From this presentation, vulnerable narcissists appear very courteous, flattering, and considerate. They want everyone to think of them as someone who's incredibly generous, polite, or virtuous.

Despite their more amenable appearance, vulnerable narcissists engage in the same antagonistic, vengeful, and superficial behaviors as any other narcissist—they simply hide it better. It's like trying to cover up a bad odor with perfume; after a while, the stench still comes through.

It's common for vulnerable narcissists to have stories about how they *would've* been the best, *should've* been more respected, or *could've* achieved so much *if only* they were born into a richer family, had better parents, got that promotion ten years ago, not been betrayed by a jealous co-worker, or any number of victimized reasons. Throughout these stories, they never take personal responsibility (or if they do, they'll say the other person's reaction was the real problem) or work to improve or change the situation. It's as if they're content to remain the perpetual victim, despite your or others' best efforts to help or encourage them.

Because vulnerable narcissists have a self-effacing, victimized persona, it can take longer to identify their behaviors as narcissistic since you're more likely to assume they're just sad and dejected. Examples of vulnerable narcissists include:

- Your withdrawn family member who consistently criticizes everyone and everything around them.

- Your friend from childhood who always calls in a panic when she needs your help even though she isn't available when you need something.

- Your co-worker who seems nice, despite having a glum demeanor. She's always having a "terrible" day, and no amount of understanding or empathy makes her feel any better.

RECOGNIZING VULNERABLE NARCISSISTS BASED ON HOW YOU FEEL

"I thought he was charming, charismatic, a little shy, and had the right intentions. He told me he was abused by his ex, so any poor behavior I saw I attributed to that. Any lies I caught ... I thought were because of the controlling ex, and I'd try and comfort him. He seemed generous and spontaneous."

–E

Relationships with vulnerable narcissists are filled with contradictions—you have to support them, but you can't outshine them; you have to take care of them, but you can't ask them to work toward self-sufficiency. These unrealistic expectations leave you feeling stuck, overwhelmed, and engulfed in their never-ending list of problems.

The main emotions you feel when dealing with a vulnerable narcissist are guilt and pity. Vulnerable narcissists manipulate you into feeling sorry for them or guilt you into helping them. You end up believing that they're simply going through a rough time and that with the right support, care, and love, they would blossom into the wonderful person you're convinced that they are.

If you're a helper, you'll feel *drawn in* by the vulnerable narcissist's stories of unfair treatment and sad, painful past. And this is exactly what makes vulnerable narcissists so dangerous: you don't suspect that their gloomy demeanor is an act of manipulation, so they feel harmless. Your defenses are down, your heart is open, and your mind is susceptible to believing in their misfortunes.

Some vulnerable narcissists even accentuate what would generally be considered embarrassing or awkward: struggling to keep a job, not being able to make their rent payments, living out of their car, flunking out of school, or not knowing how to do basic daily living tasks.

While any of us might experience these difficulties at one time or another, vulnerable narcissists use these situations to gain attention, sympathy, and control. They feel entitled to people's help, whether that be through resources, financial gain, or time. However, they don't use the help given to them to fix the problem; rather, they use it as narcissistic supply to validate to themselves how special and deserving they are.

When you feel taken advantage of, confused as to why your help doesn't seem to be making things any better, or consistently *pulled* to save someone ... pay attention! These are warning signs that you're dealing with a vulnerable narcissist.

SELF-RIGHTEOUS NARCISSISTS

Self-righteous narcissists[3] are rigid, demanding, controlling, and hyper-moralistic. Although they have a very strict sense of right and wrong, this only applies to specific issues or situations. For example, a self-righteous narcissist might have an exceptionally dogmatic view on alcohol, saying something like, "I would never lower myself to engage in such debased behavior."

At the same time, this person could be hiding a secret porn addiction and justify it by saying to themselves, "I'm not putting anyone in danger," or "What someone doesn't know can't hurt them." Hypocrisy and entitlement are part of a narcissist's makeup, and the self-righteous narcissist raises them to an art form.

Self-righteous narcissists come across as morally superior and ethically conscious. They're very judgmental and critical of those who don't meet their standards and often speak using *us* vs. *them* language.

They can be very active in religious spaces or non-profit organizations, as these environments allow them to espouse their hypocritical and entitled judgments in politically correct ways. Self-righteous narcissists *overly* identify with grand or global missions, as if what they're involved in is of far greater importance than what other people do.

Self-righteous narcissists often live very structured lives, adhering to strict routines and engaging in over-the-top behaviors in cleanliness, orderliness, and uniformity. By living in such a controlled way, they're able to prove to themselves how much better they are than everyone else, whether by how organized their towels are or how productive they are at work.

Their contempt shines through an unemotional exterior as they coldly invalidate and snub their nose at basic human emotions or authentic vulnerability. They meet their ego needs by acting morally better than those around them and pointing out others' flaws or mistakes.

Although these types of narcissists can be incredibly methodical and systematic, there's an edge of fragility to them, as if their rage could bubble to the surface the second their expectations aren't met.

Examples of self-righteous narcissists include:

- The extremely religious church member who's always looking down on those he/she considers morally reprehensible.

- The husband who insists he's a good guy because he would never cheat like other men, although he treats his spouse with contempt every day.

- The mother who yells at her children for the smallest things, like having a toy on the floor, and criticizes her five-year-old for being "messy" and "lazy."

RECOGNIZING SELF-RIGHTEOUS NARCISSISTS
BASED ON HOW YOU FEEL

"I felt like I had to be perfect. I became extremely self-conscious, aware of every move I made, knowing he was silently judging how I looked at every moment. He was very critical and demanding, especially when he didn't get his way. He would start out asking for something in a very subdued, humble manner. But if I couldn't do

what he wanted right then, it's like a switch flipped. He became
rageful, demanding I help him immediately and calling me selfish
and cold-hearted if I didn't. Even before I recognized he was a
narcissist, I knew this behavior was immature and entitled,
especially for a grown man."
                           –Brooke

Because self-righteous narcissists are so intent on controlling their world, people can mistake them for being mature, disciplined, moral, and responsible. This can make being with a self-righteous narcissist especially isolating since people often view you as lucky for being with such a "good" and "loyal" person.

However, from the inside of the relationship, it feels cold, unsettling, isolating, and unnerving. You feel like you're walking on eggshells, as you're constantly being judged, criticized, and looked upon with disgust or contempt. It's common to feel extremely self-conscious and to develop perfectionistic or compulsive behaviors as you try to cope with the narcissist's unreasonable and unrelenting standards.

In the presence of a self-righteous narcissist, even as an adult, you feel like a scolded child who's being reprimanded for minor or trivial things. They accuse you of not eating healthy enough, not working hard enough, not getting up early enough, or not being disciplined enough. They have no tolerance for bad days or bad luck and will tell you that you're being "weak," "pathetic," "lazy," or "selfish" for even trying to explain the context of your behaviors.

You begin to feel like a robot, never stepping out of line or being human at all since there's absolutely no room in this relationship for joy, humor, silliness, or fun. This kind of tense environment leaves you feeling confused, ashamed, and on edge, as if you're living in a glass box that could break at any moment.

NEGLECTFUL NARCISSISTS

Neglectful narcissists[4] appear void, hollow, and detached. Although they have all the core narcissistic traits, like entitlement, superficiality, and minimal empathy, these traits aren't as evident as with the other types. For example, while grandiose narcissists feel entitled to demand their way, neglectful narcissists feel *entitled* to ignore you.

Within intimate relationships, they come across as cold, uncaring, callous, and checked out. They might be physically present but emotionally and mentally absent. Neglectful narcissists excel at using subtle, manipulative tactics like contemptuous or disgusted snarls, blank stares, annoyed glances, resounding scoffs, and hollow conversations. Withholding behaviors, like the silent treatment, not giving you compliments, or restricting physical intimacy, are their most used manipulative strategies.

They aren't overly jealous, obsessively fixated on getting your attention, or highly controlling. They aren't likely to attack you with a verbal barrage of gaslighting, criticisms, or put-downs. They simply *don't* engage with you at all.

Neglectful narcissists often gain narcissistic supply through work, status, money, or seeking approval from a select few. Because of this, neglectful narcissists might be engaging and communicative at work and yet completely ignore their partner when they get home.

This is because they view relationships as highly transactional. They use people as pawns or conveniences to get what they want until they no longer need them, at which point they mentally and emotionally discard people until they need them again.

Being in a relationship with a neglectful narcissist can be especially tense because you don't even get to have the argument—you just get silence.

Examples of neglectful narcissists include:

- The co-parent who isn't interested at all in spending time with the kids, except when it's convenient or interesting to him/her.

- The father who values his job over everything else and is only interested in his kids' activities when it's something he can brag about to his colleagues.

- The spouse who acts as if you're invisible but says you should be grateful because they don't hit you, so you can't call them abusive.

RECOGNIZING NEGLECTFUL NARCISSISTS BASED ON HOW YOU FEEL

"I knew there was a coldness about him from the very first date. But as a very empathic person, I just thought he was misunderstood or not loved enough. I would try to do everything I could to please him, but it was never enough. It was never done the right way. I never made the right choices. I tried many different ways to show my love for him, but it was met with entitlement and superiority. It was like he thought he should be treated like a king. He would look right through me when I was speaking as if nothing I said mattered. I slowly began to feel invisible until I noticed one day that I wished I was invisible. I lost myself in that relationship, and it's taken me years to start to see glimpses of who I used to be. Although I'll never be the same, I hope one day I will feel more confident in myself again."

—Emma

When you're with a neglectful narcissist, you feel like you're emotionally suffocating. You feel overlooked, ignored, disregarded, and dismissed. You feel as though your partner views you as worthless, except when they want or need something from you, like cooking or cleaning for them, presenting yourself as a happy couple at work events, or being available for sex. You describe your relationship as hollow, empty, and void of intimacy.

Due to the amount of neglect and overall lack of regard for you as a human being in these relationships, it's not uncommon to experience symptoms of anxiety or depression. You might notice changes in your sleep, eating patterns, or general mood. You can experience a sense of discontentment about life or a loss of interest in things you used to enjoy.

You might feel apathetic, restless, irritable, or find yourself constantly ruminating about the relationship and your interactions or exchanges with your partner. Social isolation and problems in concentration can also occur.

You might feel extremely anxious and panicky at times, especially when you're being ignored or given the silent treatment. Your attempts to talk things out or resolve conflicts are met with blank stares or comments about how you want too much, are ungrateful, or can never be satisfied.

If you were abused, neglected, or overlooked in your household growing up, being treated like this again in adulthood can be excruciatingly painful, as it triggers the same feelings of abandonment, invisibility, and insignificance.

Neglectful narcissists show their contempt by meeting your pain, emotions, and tears with silence, vacant expressions, or isolation, so you become conditioned to dampen or disregard your own feelings, even when you're by yourself. You learn that your wants, needs, thoughts, or feelings are not only irrelevant to the narcissist—they're an inconvenience.

COMMUNAL NARCISSISTS

Communal narcissists[5] are very involved in charitable work, nonprofit organizations, and volunteer opportunities. They're the philanthropists and humanitarians focused on saving the world one meal or recycled water bottle at a time. They give back to their communities, lead animal rescue efforts, and show up at every school bake sale, PTO meeting, and fundraiser.

And although these activities are *good* ... communal narcissists aren't giving their efforts to these causes for the sake of doing *good*. They're doing it for the *validation* they expect to receive because of it. And if they *don't* get the applause they're looking for ... watch out. They will become irritable, angry, sullen, or lash out at those closest to them.

Communal narcissists only give their time, effort, and money if they have an audience to praise them for it or if they can document it and share it later. For example, they'll make big donations during the school's auction so they can simultaneously appear rich and giving. They'll post movie-star-quality selfies of their Saturday morning volunteering at the local soup kitchen or animal shelter.

To the outside world, communal narcissists can look saint-like since they work tirelessly to present an incredibly generous, self-sacrificing image of themselves.

However, to those closest to them, communal narcissists exhibit all the typical narcissistic traits, including being difficult, entitled, manipulative, belittling, and antagonistic. This can be incredibly disorienting, confusing, and frustrating since the world sees a completely different version of the narcissist than you do. *You* see the real version—not the constructed, distorted image everyone else gets.

Examples of communal narcissists include:

- The philanthropist who crafts his social media page to look like an advertisement for a non-profit organization.

- The mother who volunteers for every school event, fundraiser, community need, and bake sale but at home is critical, demeaning, and cold to her children and spouse.

- The church leader who volunteers his time teaching classes, staying late, and helping the sick but at home is insensitive, critical, rude, and doesn't follow the practices of his religion except in public spaces.

RECOGNIZING COMMUNAL NARCISSISTS BASED ON HOW YOU FEEL

"He seemed to be the one I'd waited my whole life for ... I felt like we were a true match; he seemed to be a good dad to his boy; he seemed to be legitimate around his parents. He would do all the chivalrous things—open doors, pay for everything, take photos everywhere we went, and wanted to post about me pretty soon on social media ... I admired his desire to serve our country ... I thought he was kind and empathetic, compassionate and generous ... During his time away, we seemed to become fully engaged in a vintage love in a modern world, old school letter writing summer love affair ... Through these letters, we decided to 'elope' when I went to see him graduate from basic training. I really thought I had prayerfully considered this ... It didn't feel wrong or rushed in any way, though when we signed the marriage license in the UPS store

on base, it was 16 weeks since we'd met. And that trip, after we signed, I started noticing some things ... and so did his mom, come to find out. He moved on to his next phase of training in yet another state, and things unraveled from there."
–Anonymous

Because you initially believe communal narcissists are nice, caring, and service-oriented, it's not uncommon to think, *"This guy (or girl) is a great catch!"* In fact, you'll often be told how lucky you are to be with such a philanthropic person or how grateful you must be to have such a kind, giving partner. However, over time, all narcissists lose their charming or humanitarian façade and become antagonistic, belittling, and critical.

When you're the partner of a communal narcissist, you notice a big difference in how they act at home vs. in public. To see the almost immediate shift in their facial expression, mood, and tone of voice when the doors close can be highly unsettling.

You might attempt to rationalize this contradiction with thoughts like, *"They do so much for others, they're probably just exhausted, and that's why they yelled at me,"* or *"I know they have such a big heart; it's probably me, I ask for too much."*

You wonder how this person who treats you so poorly can do so much good for the community or outside causes. But this is because communal narcissists can display *cognitive* empathy (i.e., intellectually understanding and caring about *concepts* like world hunger or those impacted by war zones), not *affective* empathy (i.e., having compassion for how their behaviors impact others).

Communal narcissists aren't engaging in good works out of compassion—they're doing it for validation and narcissistic supply. And because they don't receive any narcissistic supply by providing you empathy ... they don't do it. It's not about you or what you deserve—it's about their need for attention and validation.

MALIGNANT NARCISSISTS

Malignant narcissists[6] represent the darkest and most sadistic type of narcissist. They're said to be the pinnacle of the dark triad,[7] the point at which narcissism, psychopathy (i.e., antisocial behaviors), and Machiavellianism (i.e., a singular focus on power) collide. If someone is highly narcissistic, exploitative, calculating, non-empathetic, and driven to gain power without regard to how they achieve it—they're a *malignant narcissist*.

Malignant narcissists look a lot like grandiose narcissists, although they have a more intense and sinister feel to them. Their main source of supply comes from feeling dominant and superior. They want to win at all costs, even if that means engaging in unethical or illegal behavior or putting others in harm's way. They're dishonest, callous, and calculating. They don't just feel *entitled* to say and do what they want—they take *pleasure* in hurting you since they see *your pain as proof of their power*.

If you ever get in their way, disagree with them (especially in public), threaten them, or somehow displease them, they will *never* forget it. They can become fixated on seeking retribution, singularly focused on destroying your reputation, dragging you through a long, expensive legal battle, publicly humiliating you, or thwarting your attempts to advance in your career.

Examples of malignant narcissists include:

- Your ex-spouse who fights for custody of the kids not because he wants the kids but because doing so will hurt you.

- The highly respected CEO who's secretly embezzling millions of dollars to fill his pockets, even though it's going to destroy the company and hundreds of people will lose their jobs.

- The serial cheater who has sex with her affair partners in your own home and threatens to destroy your reputation if you ever divorce her or tell anyone about her affairs.

RECOGNIZING MALIGNANT NARCISSISTS BASED ON HOW YOU FEEL

"Everything was almost too good to be true for the first six months. He was literally everything that I needed and wanted. Then about a year in, I noticed how much he lied. I had never caught him in a lie to me, but I could hear him in conversations with others or on the phone, and he was always stretching the truth or flat-out lying. When I asked him about it, he treated me as if I was making a big deal out of nothing ... He led me to believe he shared the same values as me and slowly turned into someone who had no problem lying, stealing, or cheating to get ahead in business or for money ... He always made me feel as though every argument or disagreement was my fault ... He told me frequently that 'nobody else could put up with me.' My first husband had been abusive, and he said, 'I understand why he hit you' on more than one occasion. Then he would praise himself to me and say, 'at least I never hit you'... I felt worthless ... I was afraid that no one would ever love me like he did. Now I pray that no one ever does."
–Kelli

When you first encounter malignant narcissists, you feel swept away by their charm and swagger. Because they're so focused on power and dominance, they can appear incredibly poised and self-reliant.

However, over time, their passionate intensity shifts to fanatical domination as their desire to control you grows stronger. You become increasingly concerned not only about their manipulations, deceit, and control but also about their patterns of suspiciousness and paranoia. You wonder if they have a mental illness because they seem so out of touch with reality.

They ask you to share pictures of what you're doing, always want to know who you're with, or request that you turn on your GPS location so they can know where you are "in case anything happens." They frame their requests as coming from a place of concern about your safety or deep investment in knowing more about you, although you feel like these requests are more like commands.

If you express feeling like their attention is too much or too intense, they will cleverly dismiss your boundaries with a mix of flattery and guilt-tripping, explaining their intensity toward you as a sign of their deep love, affection, and care for you.

You might even start engaging in seemingly paranoid behaviors yourself, checking to see if there are hidden cameras in the house or making sure your car hasn't been tampered with before you drive it. When talking to them, you watch for signs of subtle smirks or momentary slips where you could gain insight as to what their plans are for you or the relationship.

You feel scared, hypervigilant, unsettled, and threatened, not sure how far they'll go or what they'll do if you don't meet their expectations or fall out of line. Their calculating coldness and singular focus on power affect every part of your nervous system. It's as if your body senses the presence of darkness, even if your logical mind hasn't identified the source of the threat yet.

WRAPPING UP NARCISSISTIC TYPES

By highlighting the nuances of narcissistic types, we see how different they *look* and *feel*, even though they all share the same core traits. Now that you know exactly what a narcissist is and six different types, it's time to turn our attention toward understanding *how* narcissists use these traits to harm others by exploring the narcissistic cycle of abuse.

CHAPTER FOUR

The Narcissistic Cycle of Abuse: Idealize, Devalue, Discard, Hoover

"I always said I felt like I was on a rollercoaster of a relationship. We would go up, and everything would be great. We were the 'perfect couple,' and all of a sudden, with no warning, the bottom would drop out, and I would spend weeks crying and begging for forgiveness for what I didn't know."
–Tonya

When you begin a relationship with a narcissist, you enter a game you never intended to play. While you're genuinely looking for a companion to share your life with, narcissists are looking for supply in the form of a partner. Essentially, you're being evaluated for what you can *give* to the narcissist, not who you *are*.

In the beginning of a narcissistic relationship, it often feels far from sinister or toxic. In fact, it can feel quite romantic, special, even magical. And that's exactly what the first phase of the narcissistic cycle of abuse is meant to feel like.

Let's take a wide-angle view of the narcissistic cycle of abuse, then we'll break down each phase in more detail.

The narcissistic cycle of abuse[1] has four phases: idealize, devalue, discard, and hoover. The *idealize phase* (also called love bombing) is full of excitement, hope, grandiose gestures, intensity, and feelings of infatuation, love, and adoration.

The *devalue phase* happens as the newness of the relationship wears off. Narcissists begin to be more critical, dismissive, contemptuous, and distracted. This phase is full of manipulation, belittling, gaslighting, triangulation, and boundary violations, and it can even include physical abuse, threats, or blackmail.

The *discard phase* has two options. In option one, narcissists decide to completely leave the relationship. In option two, narcissists decide to stay in the relationship but act in ways that are highly disrespectful to *emotionally* discard you without physically leaving the relationship.

After the discard phase, some narcissists completely end contact with their partner and never try to get him/her back. However, some narcissists continue the cycle of abuse with the *hoover phase*. This phase also has two possible outcomes. One, the narcissist tries to get back into a relationship with you. Or two, the narcissist maintains contact with you with no intention of getting back into a relationship.

It's important to note that this cycle characterizes the relationship from beginning to end and cycles throughout the relationship. This means narcissists can idealize, devalue, discard, and hoover you all in the same day or week. For example, you might spend a wonderful day together on Saturday, be criticized and demeaned on Sunday, given the silent treatment on Monday, and be surprised with flowers on Tuesday.

For purposes of clarity, I describe the big-picture cycle of abuse below to help you make sense of the overarching themes in these relationships. The cycle described here will make the most sense if your relationship was with a grandiose narcissist. If you feel like the description below, especially the idealize phase, doesn't really fit your relationship, this probably means you were with a different narcissistic type. In the next chapter, I explain how the idealize phase looks different with each type.

IDEALIZE PHASE

"It was unlike anything I had ever felt before in a relationship ... People would always comment about how he was so in love with me that there was nothing he wouldn't do for me. I had never had anyone treat me that way. I was over the moon. I thought this was the one, and he was my one true love. I thought of him as my knight in shining armor."
–Ronni

"We met at a local restaurant with friends. She said she knew, at first sight, I would be her husband. We had a connection because we had gone to the same college. She love bombed me, although I didn't know that term or what that was, said she liked everything I liked and insisted on spending all our time together. Pretty early in the relationship, she said we were perfect together and should get married. We married just a year after meeting."
–Sam

The idealize phase is frequently called the love bombing phase due to its intensity and fast-moving pace. It has a *mysterious* or *enchanting* air to it. You feel as if this person is too good to be true or that you share a magical connection that you can't quite put into words. There are lots of plans made about your future together and discussions about your fears, childhood memories, and hidden hopes. Although you might see a few red flags here, you'll likely overlook or dismiss them, focusing more on your emotional connection or *pull* toward them.

This phase usually lasts somewhere between a few weeks to a few months. It sets the stage for your expectation of the rest of the relationship since you feel like the connection you're developing is real and that you're genuinely getting to know this person.

However, this phase is time-limited since no relationship feels *new* forever. And for narcissists, it's the newness and excitement that puts them on their best behavior. When the relationship starts turning more serious, and your expectations for them grow (as they should), they become resentful of your needs, emotionally distant, and irritated when you share your feelings. It's at this point of the relationship that you enter the *devalue phase*.

DEVALUE PHASE

"It went from 'I'm the greatest' to 'I'm the devil' in an instant. It started with little jabs at the stupidest stuff. All things that were demeaning to me, like if I accidentally bumped into something, I was the clumsiest person ever. Then she started to do things like kick me out after making love for no reason whatsoever. Then once I calmly drew a boundary, she took it as criticism and went all in for the jugular, flipping me from the greatest to the devil."
–Robert

"This was the hardest to spot; it was subtle, and, to start with, was the use of language. It was never 'we' went on holiday; it was always 'I took' her. He started to make me look foolish in front of his family ... He shared a photo of me that he knew I disliked; he did it to get his family to laugh at me. He constantly messaged saying that he did everything he could for me but that he got nothing in return ... After I discovered he'd been flirting with multiple women

*on Instagram, I said we needed to talk about appropriate social
media communication ... I expected an apology, but what I got was
a full-on tirade of counterclaims ... I tried to calm him down, but
nothing worked—suddenly it hit me, and I called it out to him ...
'You're a narcissist!' It stopped him in his tracks; he went from this
angry, volatile, verbally abusive man to ... hurt, sad, and dejected in
an instant."*
—Evie

In this phase, the relationship temperature changes from *hot* to *cool*. You notice the connection isn't as intense as it used to be and that your partner is less responsive or attentive. You feel like you're losing their interest, as they seem more distant or distracted.

For example, they might make excuses for why they can't see you as often, noting they have to work during the evenings or on weekends, even though they never had to do this during the first few months of dating.

During the devalue phase, narcissists are inconsistent with their compliments, forget important events, or subtly criticize your hobbies, interests, clothing style, friends, food choices, or just about anything you do or say. For example, if they used to praise your spontaneity, now they say you're unpredictable and irresponsible. They take everything positive they've said about you or vulnerable feelings you've shared with them and find a way to belittle, criticize, or demean you for it.

When you start to notice this shift and ask them about it, they tell you you're being paranoid, overdramatic, or too sensitive. When you ask them what's changed, if you did something wrong, or how you can get back to the way things were, they tell you you're being controlling, that nothing has changed, and that your expectations are too high.

As this phase continues, you feel more and more confused, run-down, guilty, worthless, hypervigilant, anxious, unmotivated, discouraged, and exasperated, as you have no idea what happened or how to get back to the way things were at the beginning of the relationship.

This is the phase where you try everything: therapy, communicating differently, taking all the blame, trying to be better, smarter, more attractive, more interesting … you think if you could solve the issue, repair the damage, or figure out how to reconnect, then everything would go back to the way it was.

But the reality is there's not a *there* to get back to. What you thought was real was a façade. You can't fix a relationship that was founded on a lie.

DISCARD PHASE

"He never threatened to leave me. He had just discarded me in the marriage. I told him that I was being treated like a ghost in my own home. He would speak to me through the children, not using my name or addressing me personally at all. I would make tea and toast for him in the morning so that he would have something in his stomach before work. I would stand in the kitchen holding out the plate and cup, and he would walk directly past me, not uttering a word. He would leave through the back door, slamming it as he went. When he returned from work, he would hug and kiss the boys in a very over-the-top demonstration of affection towards them but not even acknowledge my presence. I may as well have been a ghost."
—Miss B.

"He said, 'Well, we've been married 12 years, we had a good run,'
then walked out the door to the gym with a bounce in his step and a
smile on his face! I was devastated!"
—Joanne

Discarding is the ultimate example of how narcissists view *people as pawns* to be used when they need something and thrown away when they're done. Discarding is the narcissist's way of saying, "I'm done with you," and no longer have a need for you, which is incredibly painful, hurtful, and isolating.

This phase is extremely disorienting, as you're constantly searching for answers and explanations for what's happening. You feel lost, confused, panicked, depressed, or even numb, as if you're in shock or denial. Your mind races with flashes of the "good times" as you try to figure out what went wrong, if there was something you could've done differently, or how you missed the warning signs.

Discarding can trigger feelings of abandonment, harm, and danger, which activates the body's fight, flight, freeze, or fawn response. This means all the physiological symptoms, emotions, and physical changes that occur when you're in danger can happen during this phase as well.

As mentioned previously, discarding can happen emotionally or physically. Regardless of the type of discard, *you feel thrown away, tossed to the side, and utterly rejected.*

If the narcissist discards you by *physically* leaving the relationship, you experience a range of emotions. Some people feel depressed, empty, anxious, or deeply lonely, and some people feel relieved, although most experience a combination of all these.

Your emotional reaction depends largely on how long the devalue phase lasted and how aware you are of the fact that you're in a narcissistic relationship. If you've been in the devalue phase for quite some time, then part of you might have expected the discard phase, even if you didn't necessarily call it that. However, some people are completely blindsided when the narcissist leaves the relationship.

If the narcissist emotionally discards you but *stays* in the relationship, you feel as if you're a ghost. They give you long-lasting silent treatments, cheat on you, completely disregard you when making decisions that impact you (e.g., taking a new job that requires moving), or become incredibly cold and callous.

Something eerie can happen when narcissists discard you—they start telling the truth. They leave clues for you to figure out what they're up to. It's like they want to get caught so it can all be out in the open and over.

They stop love bombing you. They stop future faking you. They stop hoovering you. And they start being more open about what they want—even if they know you'll never agree to it.

They say things like, "I want an open marriage," "I'm cheating on you," "I'm not coming home tonight," "We're not making any more plans together," "I can't give you what you want," "You'd be happier with someone else," or "Why don't you just leave?"

This shift can be really overwhelming and even scary because nothing makes sense anymore. Not that it ever really did—but you got used to them hiding, lying, and manipulating. And now ... they don't even put in the effort to hide their deceit.

You start to wonder, *"Did I ever even know this person at all?"*

WHAT TRIGGERS THE DISCARD PHASE?

The discard phase is fueled[2] by a mix of boredom, contempt, and entitlement. Narcissists are incredibly novelty-seeking, meaning they become easily bored and want something new to entertain them. They're always seeking external validation to make themselves feel good and to regulate their emotions. That's why many of them are motivated to eventually discard their partner, only to begin the narcissistic cycle of abuse again with a new person.

Narcissists are full of contempt not just for their own and others' emotions but also for authentic intimacy or connection. As the relationship progresses and intimacy *should* be developing, narcissists become uncomfortable with this expected emotional closeness, and they blame *you* as the reason they're feeling so uncomfortable. This, too, motivates narcissists to find a new partner who doesn't have so many expectations for them.

Finally, narcissists' entitlement means they believe they should get what they want, when they want, how they want. They have little to no concern for how you will feel during the discard. They're focused on doing what makes *them* happy, and getting fresh narcissistic supply is a surefire way to do that, at least in the short term.

HOOVERING

"I remember never having felt more desired in my life. I felt like the luckiest man in the world. I realized though, that she never seemed happy with anything I tried to do. I eventually broke off our engagement. She was furious. About six months later, she asked that we meet to get some closure. I wanted her to be able to heal. After dinner, she absolutely seduced me. That weekend, she convinced me I had made a mistake but that she would forgive me."
–David

Hoovering is the process by which narcissists attempt to smooth over relationship difficulties or maintain communication with you after a breakup. Hoovering can happen whether you left the narcissist, or the narcissist left you. While not *all* narcissists hoover, it happens more often than not.

This is because hoovering, in and of itself, is a form of narcissistic supply. If you still talk to them, despite how they treated you or your relationship status, it feeds their ego. It's not uncommon for narcissists to stay in contact with several ex-partners. In their mind, open communication means you still want them.

Narcissists hoover using many of the same techniques they employ at the beginning of the relationship: charm, charisma, grand gestures, love bombing, sweet texts or gifts, guilt-tripping, or a combination of all these. But this time around, they have an advantage: *their knowledge of you and your previous attachment to them.*

Consider Chelsea's story of narcissistic abuse and how her partner hoovered her back into the relationship:

> *"[At first] he was very attentive. He listened and was affectionate and caring. He mostly agreed with everything I said and told me I was 'perfect.' When I said I wasn't, he would say, 'perfect for him.' I would catch him staring at me with a grin and googly eyes. He would say I was the love of his life, his angel that God sent to him, that we were made for each other. I always told him he needed to take his rose-colored glasses off. We would dance in the kitchen while listening to music, make love often and passionately, he would take me to nice restaurants and just do special things with me like ride bikes, take walks, show me a new site or park in the area.*

This (devalue) phase grew over time. I didn't even realize I was being devalued, but there became a time when suddenly everything changed (although slowly, it felt sudden to me). I wasn't 'perfect' any longer ... The things I said or believed in that he once would have agreed with were now wrong; everything I said was wrong. No matter what it was. I couldn't do anything right! The discard process felt like it happened many times. He would say we were done over and over and tell me horrible things. He would then call the next day saying he can't live without me, and he was going to prove his love to me ... He would call, email in whatever way he could that he wasn't blocked from. Beg me to please talk to him until I would cave. He would send me flowers with love notes. I was only able to succeed with no contact for 48 hours, two times only. The trauma bond was strong. I thought that was it. It wasn't. I somehow got sucked back in."

Another narcissistic abuse survivor shared how her mother tried to hoover her back into more contact:

"This is the phase that I'm currently in with my mother. I began therapy about seven months ago and started putting much-needed boundaries in place. At first, my mother would send messages like, 'If you think I've done anything to hurt you, I'm sorry...' Now I receive more messages like, 'I love you—I'd love to see you all' or questions about when she can get my kids or their activity schedules. She'll post things to social media about my kids—like birthday posts or memories but won't call them. Holidays are approaching, and she's been asking me about dates, which I've tried to

ignore or pass off. I can tell she knows boundaries have been put into place and think she's trying to guilt trip me into tearing them down. She's always bragged to others that I'm a people pleaser and I can't keep anything from her."

Narcissistic hoovering is no joke. It can feel even stronger and more powerful than the initial love bombing phase because you have a history with this person. The narcissist knows you better now. They know your strengths and weaknesses, your firm convictions, and your values. They know what you wanted from them and didn't get. Because they know all these things, they can manipulate you *now* in ways they couldn't before.

DOES A NARCISSIST EVER *NOT* HOOVER?

If a narcissist *doesn't* try to hoover you, it's likely for one of two reasons: they're distracted with new narcissistic supply, or you became too difficult to control. If narcissists sense that someone has firm boundaries, will call them out on their inconsistencies, and isn't easily manipulated, they will move on to an easier target.

Likewise, if they're trying to win over new supply, they might not put energy into something that's "old news" in their mind.

Whether they hoover you or not, here's what you can know with absolute certainty: it has nothing to do with *you* and everything to do with *them*. Narcissists are self-serving and do whatever is most convenient for them, regardless of the impact it has on you or anyone else.

WRAPPING UP THE CYCLE OF ABUSE

All narcissists follow some version of the idealize, devalue, discard, and hoover cycle. While the devalue, discard, and hoover phases look similar across the types, the idealize phase can feel *much different* depending on the type of narcissist you're dealing with. The next chapter breaks down what it *looks like* and *feels like* to be love bombed by each narcissistic type.

CHAPTER FIVE

Narcissistic Love Bombing: How Different Types Do It

"When we were dating, he was very attentive. He treated me like a queen the majority of the time. Looking back, it almost felt like he worshiped the ground I walked on. He wanted to be together all the time. He opened up his wallet to plan trips and experiences for us. He made me feel seen, valued, and loved. Occasionally there would be interactions that did not fit this narrative, but at the time they felt like the exception, the outlier. Not like red flags."
—Beth

I want you to think about something.

Regarding relationships … what are your deepest desires? Do you have a strong desire to be needed? Do you long to be cherished and adored? Do you crave consistency and predictability?

The reason narcissistic love bombing is so effective is because it speaks to your unmet needs. Whatever you want *most* is often what you *think* you're getting with a narcissist.

If you want to feel needed, you'll be most susceptible to the vulnerable narcissist's love bombing style. If you want to feel cherished, you'll be most susceptible to the grandiose narcissist's love bombing style. If you want structure and predictability, you'll be most susceptible to the self-righteous narcissist's love bombing style.

While none of these needs or wants are bad or wrong (and we'll explore how to get these needs met in a healthy way in later chapters), it's important to be aware of them so you're not as easily charmed by the narcissist's illusions. *You will never find what you want by falling for a narcissist's promises*. Because as soon as you believe in them, they disappear. Narcissists are nightmares masquerading as daydreams.

LOVE BOMBED BY A GRANDIOSE NARCISSIST

Grandiose narcissists follow the typical idealize phase as discussed in the previous chapter. They love bomb you with flattery, charm, gifts, time, and attention. They learn about you by taking an interest in your hobbies and asking about your favorite songs, preferred vacation spots, and important aspirations. They become (for a time) everything you ever wanted.

Although grandiose narcissists lavish you with attention, surprises, and make you feel "special," a lot of the conversations center around *them*. They tell you about their successes, achievements, and grandiose plans for the future. Essentially, they market themselves as an "award-winning product" or "prized possession" that *you* are lucky enough to be with.

While being love bombed by a grandiose narcissist, many people report feeling swept away, enchanted, and completely charmed or enamored.

LOVE BOMBED BY A VULNERABLE NARCISSIST

The idealize phase is about drawing you in, whether through grandiose gestures of love (as the grandiose narcissist does) or guilt trips and opportunities to help (as the vulnerable narcissist does). Early in the relationship, vulnerable narcissists tend to overshare about their struggles, ups and downs, difficult past relationships, or ways people have let them down, treated them unfairly, or been cruel.[1]

Although you might assume they're just sharing about their life, these revelations come too fast, too soon. You leave these conversations feeling exceptionally sorry for them, and before you know it, you're adjusting your calendar, moving your plans, and overlooking your obligations to meet *their* needs.

Vulnerable narcissists love bomb by gaining your sympathy, pity, and saying things like:

- "You saved my life; I don't know what I would do without you."

- "I don't deserve you; you're so incredible! I can't believe you're with me."

- "I know you would never leave me. I don't know what I would do if I felt that lonely again."

- "My parents never supported my entrepreneurial ideas. If someone just believed in me and supported me financially until I could get my business off the ground, I could really be successful."

- "You're exactly what I need. You make me feel so good about myself."

At first glance, these statements seem sincere and sweet. But when used by a narcissist, they're incredibly effective at manipulating your emotions and behaviors. These statements subtly imply that *you* are the reason the narcissist is okay and that if you ever left, *you* would be responsible for causing them great harm.

These menacingly manipulative messages are especially effective for people who grew up in toxic environments, are highly empathetic or compassionate, struggle with low self-worth, have loose boundaries, are perpetually drawn toward helper roles, or were raised by a narcissistic parent.

In short, you know you've been love bombed by a vulnerable narcissist when you stop helping them out of choice and start helping them out of obligation.

LOVE BOMBED BY A SELF-RIGHTEOUS NARCISSIST

Self-righteous narcissists are excellent rule-followers, as they gain narcissistic supply from doing everything the "right" way and by being morally superior. If you're looking for someone who holds a certain moral standard, practices a particular religion, or will fit into the cultural expectations of your family, then you'll likely be drawn toward a person who is very loyal or committed in those areas.

Self-righteous narcissists use their strict ethical guidelines and rigidly structured life to love bomb[2] their target into believing that they're trustworthy, dependable, and honest. For example, you assume that because they're heavily involved in church, have a consistent personal development routine, or keep a very tidy house that they will be loyal, responsible, and consistent.

This type of love bombing is alluring and comforting to those who grew up in chaotic homes, are used to dysfunctional relationships, or have been burned by people who are irresponsible or lax on rules, values, or ethical behavior.

LOVE BOMBED BY A COMMUNAL NARCISSIST

Communal narcissists love bomb[3] in much the same way they gain narcissistic supply—by portraying themselves as humble, giving, selfless people whose only goal in life is to make a difference in the world. They purposefully tell you about the charities they've donated to, benefits they've attended, and causes they're involved in.

They make you think they *are* their image. They communicate in such a self-effacing way that their accomplishments don't come across as arrogant but as unassuming, genuine, and compassionate.

Because being viewed as *selfless* is a huge part of communal narcissists' ground game, you initially feel safe with them. You feel special, even lucky, to be with such a kindhearted and giving person. You mistakenly (although understandably) believe that their outwardly good deeds come from a genuinely benevolent heart.

LOVE BOMBED BY A MALIGNANT NARCISSIST

Being love bombed by a malignant narcissist feels enchanting, alluring, intense, and passionate.[4] They are considerably complimentary and fixated on gaining your approval, attention, and admiration. They come across as *very* into you, asking countless questions about your likes, dislikes, hopes, and dreams. They send lots of texts and want to be in constant contact. You might be surprised at the amount of attention you're getting, feeling as if it's flattering but also too much at times.

Many malignant narcissists are highly successful, which means they have the resources and money to create a fairytale romance. They take you on trips, fly you across the country, or lavish you with expensive gifts. They offer to take care of you financially while you go back to school, insist that you move in with them, or pay off debts that you can't repay. Regardless of the action, their goal for the love bombing phase is to make you dependent on them and feel obligated to adjust your life to accommodate their schedule and needs.

LOVE BOMBED BY A NEGLECTFUL NARCISSIST

Of all the narcissistic types, the neglectful narcissist has the most understated idealize phase. Many times, people are love bombed by neglectful narcissists not by flattery or charm but by convenience or practicality.[5] In other words, you're drawn to them and stay in the relationship because it "makes sense" (e.g., you're getting older and want to get married).

Neglectful narcissists don't do much to win you over. But they are good at showing up during transitional moments, like when you get divorced, move to a new city, or have a falling out with a friend.

If you've been hurt in relationships by loud, controlling types, you might try (consciously or subconsciously) to keep yourself emotionally safe by finding someone who isn't so intense. You might have thoughts like, *"I never want to have my heart broken like that again,"* or *"I'll never let myself be the one who cares more in the relationship."*

These situations make neglectful narcissists seem like a safe bet since their love bombing style is missing the intensity or grandiosity that characterizes typical love bombing. Then, once you've been in the relationship for a while, you end up feeling stuck or like you've invested so much in the relationship you don't want to have "wasted" all that time—so you stay.

WRAPPING UP LOVE BOMBING BY NARCISSISTIC TYPES

Being idealized, devalued, discarded, and hoovered creates a hurricane-sized wave of emotions and feels messy, confusing, overwhelming, frustrating, heartbreaking, and debilitating. It makes you question everything you thought you knew about communication, love, sex, and what it takes to make a relationship work.

But even if you recognize and understand the narcissistic cycle of abuse, there's a lot more to unravel about these relationships. Questions and thoughts like, *"Why do I never feel good enough?" "Is there something wrong with me?" "The relationship is over. Why can't I move on?" "Am I going crazy?" "No matter what I do, I can't win,"* or *"I overthink everything! Why can't I stop ruminating?"* still linger in your mind.

And that's why understanding not just the cycle, but also narcissistic abuse is so important. If the narcissistic cycle is the shell, then narcissistic abuse is the material the shell is made of. It's in every fiber of the relationship and affects you psychologically, emotionally, physically, and spiritually. The next chapter unravels the layers of narcissistic abuse.

CHAPTER SIX

Narcissistic Abuse: Uncovering the Layers of Deception and Chaos

"He would say things that were unkind and excuse it as a joke. I was starting to feel like I had to beg for his time or pencil myself into his schedule. He started using our different upbringings in arguments. He never had anything and thought I had it so much better than him. Failures were always someone else's fault. He was always the victim. There was never any accountability ... I avoided things or let things slide just to keep the peace. He told me many times I needed to see a doctor. I started to think maybe I was the problem. Is what I'm doing causing him to treat me this way? Am I asking for too much? Am I being too critical of him? I started to feel very alone and insignificant and like I was an annoyance."
–Anonymous

Narcissistic abuse is a multilayered attack on your sense of self—a dismantling of who you are and what you believe you're worth. It includes consistent and repetitive manipulative tactics used by narcissists to meet their ego needs and gain control over your emotions, perceptions, and thoughts.[1]

These tactics include behaviors like gaslighting, minimization, lying, manipulation, exploitation, passive-aggressiveness, and can range from mild to severe. While not all narcissists engage in physical violence, the more sadistic types, particularly malignant narcissists, are certainly capable of violent and aggressive acts. Narcissistic abuse can also be financial, spiritual, and sexual in nature.[2]

Because narcissistic abuse includes a range of behaviors, it would be nearly impossible to name them all. However, below, you'll find a checklist of some of the most common abusive strategies.

- Belittling/Criticizing
- Gaslighting
- Lying
- Manipulation
- Blame-Shifting
- Passive Aggressiveness
- Contempt
- Silent Treatment
- Withholding
- Physical Abuse
- Smear Campaign

These narcissistically abusive patterns are expanded on below. You'll notice that some of these behaviors overlap. For example, gaslighting is its own abusive strategy, but it is also manipulative. Lying can happen on its own or as a part of gaslighting.

Let's break down what these patterns look like, why they're used, and how to recognize them in a relationship.

BELITTLING/CRITICIZING: WHY YOU NEVER FEEL GOOD ENOUGH

"As a kid, I simply assumed that since I was the kid, I was probably in the wrong (didn't clean my room, didn't listen well enough, etc.). But as I became a teen, I found that when I tried to express something she [my mother] was doing that was making it hard for me to relate with her, she continued to say it was because of me or that the greater fault was mine ... When she skipped my wedding reception, she never explained her absence, and when I was angry later, she said I was holding onto grievances too long, and I had always been too sensitive. The last straw was that she made some critical comments about my husband and kids, and when I confronted her and told her that the words were not respectful, she stated that she had never said any of the things I brought up, and also, I had always been too sensitive."
–Anonymous

If there's one thing narcissists are good at—it's being critical. Narcissists gain a sense of superiority by criticizing and belittling you. They make fun of your hobbies, interests, how you cook, what you watch or listen to, the way you dress, what you wear, how you talk, what you look like ... the list is endless!

Anything and everything you do, say, wear, like, or feel can and will be criticized. Even silly, irrelevant things, like the way you take a drink, the new song you like, the way you comb your hair, or your preferred brand of toothpaste, can all be ridiculed by a narcissist.

While they criticize you outright on many things, narcissists also subtly criticize you because it's more easily denied or played off as a joke. They say things like:

- "You're wearing *that*?"
- "Do *you* really need to be giving weight loss advice?"
- "Are you sure you know what you're doing?"
- "I was only asking a question, don't be so sensitive."
- "Is that the third time today you've lost your keys?"
- "I was only joking!"

NARCISSISTIC PURPOSES OF CRITICIZING

Criticisms bolster the narcissist's fragile ego since narcissists feel superior when they put others down. Being critical feeds narcissists' entitlement, as criticisms create a natural divide between you and them, making them feel special or chosen. Being critical also means the narcissist feels powerful and in control.

Narcissists use subtle criticisms when they want to put you down but also "save face" in front of a group. Subtle criticisms are harder to detect and might not be noticed at all by those outside of the relationship. This makes subtle criticisms even more damaging because it isolates you and leads you to wonder if maybe *you* are the one with the problem.

GASLIGHTING: HOW NARCISSISTS STEAL YOUR REALITY

"She would ... try and convince me that she told me to fix something or that I said I would do a certain thing when I knew this conversation never took place. But then I would apologize and start to believe that I was wrong, and we did discuss it. She emasculated me and made me feel inferior. Then she would prop me back up and love bomb me again."
–Doug

Gaslighting is a type of psychological abuse intended to confuse, manipulate, distort, and control your reality.[3] Narcissists use gaslighting to make you distrust your judgment and perpetually question your thoughts, feelings, intentions, and perceptions.

Gaslighting is a complex and sophisticated manipulation strategy because it's deceptively subtle but incredibly effective at slowly chipping away your reality and sense of self.

This is because, for gaslighting to work, the relationship must be built on a foundation of trust, familiarity, and likability. That's why the narcissistic cycle of abuse begins with love bombing—narcissists need to gain your trust before they can effectively gaslight you.

The more you form an attachment to someone, the more likely you are to believe them. For example, you're more likely to trust what a friend says than a stranger. And oftentimes, you're more likely to trust what your partner says than a friend. Unfortunately, narcissists capitalize on this and use it to make you believe you're someone you're not.

Gaslighting isn't just lying—it's lying *and* making you believe you're crazy. You've experienced this if you've ever provided a narcissist with proof of an indiscretion, inconsistency, or betrayal, and they still won't admit to it. This can feel infuriating and hopeless, as you likely went through painstaking steps to make sure you had solid evidence to prove your point.

A narcissistic abuse survivor put it like this: *"He started following inappropriate pages on Instagram and denied it with hard evidence. He accused me and actually tried to brainwash me into thinking I was insecure."*

Instead of an admission, you get reprimanded for being crazy, obsessive, difficult, selfish, controlling, or ridiculous. Narcissists do this because they don't care about what's true—they care about what they can get away with. Statements like, "That never happened," "I never said that," "You have a bad memory," "You don't know what you're talking about," or "You're crazy" are examples of obvious gaslighting.

Subtle forms of gaslighting include ignoring your perspective, constantly changing the subject, blame-shifting, acting like they didn't hear you, and projecting. For example, when you call them out on a lie, they don't address the fact that they lied. Instead, they blame-shift by changing the subject, criticize you for being so suspicious, and devalue you by acting like your questions are the real problem.

Narcissists consistently minimize your feelings or experiences by saying things like, "You have no right to feel that way," "It's not a big deal," "You're so sensitive," "You always have to get your way," or "I can't believe you're still talking about that."

They might feign caring about you while questioning your sanity at the same time with statements like, "You've been forgetting a lot lately, are you sure you're okay?" or "You seem really depressed; maybe you should get some help."

Narcissists excel at crafting seemingly loving statements with an undertone of control and devaluation by saying things like, "No one will ever love you like I do," "You'll never find anyone who cares about you this much," or "A lot of people would do anything to have the lifestyle you have with me." Narcissists don't live in the reality of truths and proofs—they live in a projected reality of their own making.

Robert recounts his experiences with gaslighting:

> "It would start very slowly and insidiously. For example, she would make dismissive and judgmental comments on things ... She would ask me very personal questions about my life experiences. Being in a relationship, a healthy person wants to become vulnerable. They want to be able to let their guard down and share any possible insecurities or challenging or traumatizing life experiences. However, she would later weaponize them against me. She would bring up these experiences in an attempt to gaslight me or make me think that something was defective or wrong with me. For example, if I would express that my feelings were hurt about some incident where she showed no empathy, she would respond by insisting it was because I grew up around poverty, or because I was a military veteran, or because I am not sleeping well. I began to have severe chronic health problems, and she would gaslight me into thinking that something was wrong with me, when in fact, my health decline was a response to her complex abuse."

Evie describes the effects of gaslighting:

> "I thought I was losing my memory. I needed to start writing down things he said to me, especially

unpleasant things, as he would deny saying them. He said I was crazy, and I started to believe it. I became more and more withdrawn and ended up diagnosed with depression and on medication."

Angela found herself questioning everything:

"He would always talk about how great he was. How everyone loved him. I was always asking myself why the relationship didn't work. I was wondering if I was crazy from the arguments being turned on me."

Gaslighting can also sound like:

- "Your silence is proof that you're guilty."

- "Nothing to say? That's what I thought. You're a coward."

- "I can't believe you kept those text messages! You're so controlling!"

- "Even your friends see how you treat me."

- "Nothing is ever good enough for you."

- "You don't really want things to get better; you just want to argue about it."

Gaslighting leaves you questioning yourself and feeling guilty, foggy, confused, and anxious. Over time, you feel more disconnected from yourself, less confident in who you are, more unsure of your feelings and needs, and less trusting of your ability to make sense of things without the narcissist's input.

To take my *Am I Being Gaslighted?* quiz, go to https://www.chelseybrookecole.com/quizzes or scan the QR code.

NARCISSISTIC PURPOSES OF GASLIGHTING

The purpose of gaslighting is to separate *you* from *your reality* so that the *narcissist* becomes the filter through which you see yourself and the world. This is because *the less you trust yourself, the easier you are to manipulate*. Gaslighting is one of, if not the most, insidious and harmful emotional abuse tactics used by narcissists. It's through the use of gaslighting that narcissists gain control of your perceptions, reality, and mental headspace.

When gaslighting reaches its full potential, your sovereignty is destroyed, as you become the narcissist's puppet—thinking, feeling, believing, and acting in whatever way they see fit. You no longer think, act, or feel for yourself because you don't even know who *you* are anymore. You feel so internally disconnected, discombobulated, disorganized, and disheveled that you struggle to make sense of things *without* the narcissist's input, even though it's *because* of the narcissist's influence that you feel unable to think for yourself.

Narcissists don't have a solid sense of self, so they seek to engulf *you* as if they're feeding and living off your existence. If they control *you*, then *they* feel powerful. If they disorient *you*, then *they* feel clear. If they unnerve *you*, then *they* feel calm. They attempt to regulate their erratic emotional world by controlling everything and everyone around them.

As with all narcissistic behaviors, *it's not about you*. It's about what the narcissist needs, wants, or craves. Narcissists reach outside of themselves and into other people's mental and emotional worlds to make themselves feel better.

Instead of looking inward and asking, *"How can I heal myself? What are my needs, and how can I meet those needs?"* they look to other people, places, or things to fill the emptiness inside of them. And gaslighting is the number one tool they use to make that happen.

LYING: THERE'S ALWAYS MORE TO THE STORY

"We had gotten into an argument, and I realized he wasn't being truthful about certain issues, and I confronted him, and he snapped. I was so scared of him that night, and the next day, he tried to gaslight me and say it was my own doing/fault for prying. He was unable to take ownership of his own faults. I had to practically beg him to apologize. He would just become very angry when I would point something out about him, and I couldn't understand."
–Valerie

There's really nothing a narcissist won't lie about if it benefits them in some way. They lie about what they do, where they go, who they're with, their job requirements, academic or career successes, hobbies, interests ... you name it—narcissists lie about it. And they most definitely lie about their past relationships and friendships, particularly regarding why those relationships ended and how they behaved in those relationships.

During the love bombing phase, you usually don't know enough about the narcissist to realize that they're lying. However, their lies become more apparent the longer you're with them, as things start *not* adding up.

Lying is typically one of the first big tells that something is seriously off about the relationship. You begin realizing that what you thought you knew about them, their history, family, career goals, and achievements, were either completely fabricated or seriously flawed.

Yet, the more you question them about these inconsistencies, the more enraged they become. The lies get bigger, the stories get grander, and their fuse becomes shorter.

Future faking is a form of lying where narcissists make promises about the future to gain something they want in the present. For example, in the beginning of the relationship, narcissists might initiate conversations about your goals as a couple to secure your commitment to the relationship.

Once you're committed to the relationship, they use future faking to convince you to stay or smooth things over after a fight, reassuring you that things will be better down the road. But as with everything involving a narcissist, it's all an illusion.

NARCISSISTIC PURPOSES OF LYING

Lying is as natural to a narcissist as breathing. It plays a central part in protecting their fragile ego, managing their image, and gaining narcissistic supply. Essentially, the viability of narcissists' way of life depends on their ability to lie to *themselves* and *others*.

Narcissists lie to themselves by refusing to look at their inconsistent and selfish behaviors, which is how they convince themselves they're a good person and that anyone who doesn't believe this is out to get them.

Narcissists lie to others by claiming their false image is real. Everything narcissists want to believe about themselves and project to the world falls apart if they tell the truth.

This is why giving narcissists proof will not change their behavior. They don't care that they're lying. Showing them proof or arguing with them will only incite their shame/rage cycle, where they will blame *you* for causing problems because you're the one calling them out.

Lying serves many narcissistic purposes, such as:

- Lying offers a quick fix for difficult issues.
- Lying is a way to avoid responsibility.
- Lying about accomplishments can create more praise.
- Lying throws people off balance.
- Lying is very self-serving.
- Lying is a source of entitlement.
- Lying is an effective manipulation strategy.

Narcissists lie because they feel entitled to do so. They lie to save face, hide things they would be judged for, and perpetuate their false image.

Narcissists aren't concerned about what's true or false. They're concerned about getting validation and feeling superior. To a narcissist, validation is always more important than the truth. And if lying gets them validation, then that's exactly what they'll do.

MANIPULATION: THE NARCISSIST'S GROUND GAME

"He started accusing me of arguing anytime I brought up something that bothered me. He was very controlling; he made me share my

location with him on my phone. He made me give up guy friendships
... He never respected my feelings. He always disregarded my
feelings saying I was 'running my mouth' ... So I learned then he
didn't care about me or my feelings, only his own, which made me
realize how selfish he is."
–Christy

No one manipulates more effectively or cunningly than a narcissist. Narcissists manipulate you, that is, seek to exploit or control you to their advantage in many ways.[4]

One of the most common ways is by mislabeling your emotions. They mislabel your anxiety as insecurity. They mislabel your anger as proof of your volatility. They mislabel your sadness as chronic depression. They mislabel your confusion as instability.

Narcissists also ignore the explanations you give for your behaviors and replace them with their own. You go for a walk at night—they accuse you of cheating. You bring up something that's bothering you—they blame you for ruining their day. You ask where they went after work—they tell you that you're crazy, obsessive, and controlling. You ask them to schedule a date night with you—they criticize you for never being satisfied. You try to address their lies or manipulations—they ask why you can't ever focus on the "good" things they do. Narcissists don't accept your explanations or intentions. Instead, they want you to accept their interpretations as fact.

Triangulation is another powerful manipulative tool. Triangulation[5] occurs when one person (in this case, the narcissist) becomes the mediator between two people. When a narcissist becomes the "go-between" person, they're able to control the narrative and effectively manipulate both parties. Since you aren't directly talking to the other person, you must trust that the narcissist is correctly interpreting and communicating the message, which inevitably, they're not.

Narcissists triangulate you in two ways: what they say to *you* about *others* and what they say to *others* about *you*. Narcissists are notorious for spreading lies about you to your friends, co-workers, acquaintances, and family members. They make up stories about how you're abusive, controlling, crazy, jealous, insecure, incompetent, or any other trait that will gain people's attention, sympathy, or validation.

Triangulation is a way for narcissists to create chaos, drama, and conflict. You know you're being triangulated when the narcissist starts telling you what other people think about you, especially when you've never been told these things directly.

Faye describes her narcissistic mother's manipulations like this:

> *"She desperately wants attention and validation and to be the victim. If you don't give her that, you get punished. At the end of the 1.5-hour conversation, she'll say, 'And how are you and the kids?' And when you have no energy left to say anything positive, she'll get cross. Over the years, she has used me and my sister as agony aunts for her marital problems with my dad (even as teenagers) and says she needs us to support her. She often plays the depressed card and wants us to be worried about her, but when we try to get her to see a doctor, she refuses. Our mum has used triangulation for as long as I remember, slagging with me, my sister, my aunt, or my dad off to one of the others and gossiping about us to each of the others."*

NARCISSISTIC PURPOSES OF MANIPULATION

By labeling your emotions and intentions, narcissists get inside your head and make you think you're going crazy. This is how they deconstruct your sense of self. They want to replace your inner voice with their own. To shape you from the inside out is the ultimate win for a narcissist because being inside your head is the most powerful place they can be.

Narcissistic triangulation serves several purposes. When narcissists talk to you about other people, they tell you what they want you to believe. For example, narcissists will claim to know secrets about your friends or family that you've never heard before (and they "can't" give away their source either). Narcissists will claim to be the only one that your friends confide in regarding their pet peeves about you.

However, it's much more likely that the narcissist made everything up; your friends never said anything bad about you, and it was all a ploy to further manipulate, gaslight, and isolate you.

Triangulation is a fundamental method used by narcissists to isolate you from your support system. Because narcissists strategically place themselves in between *you* and *others*, they successfully control the narrative. You stop believing what other people say and start believing what the narcissist *says* they say.

Katie explains how her ex used triangulation to cause harm:

> *"He triangulated people I didn't even know by talking badly about me behind my back. He also did this with family members (his and mine) and co-workers ... He made up total lies about everything and told anyone who would listen. Much of this came back to me by*

accident. He even convinced marriage counselors that
I was saying or doing things that I wasn't."

This is a very dangerous but effective way narcissists simultaneously *isolate* you from others and *normalize* their abuse since you're less likely to talk about the difficulties of your relationship with people you don't trust. Over time, this pushes you into the narcissist's bubble, where *their* reality becomes *your* reality. And a narcissist's reality is a very treacherous place to be.

BLAME-SHIFTING: IT'S ALWAYS YOUR FAULT

"At home, she would nit-pick everyone, especially me and my son. She was extremely moody. She set the tone and mood of our home. Everything had to be in its place, to her liking. She would blame me for everything, and little by little, I began to always try and stay ahead of her to make sure everything was done to her liking. If we got into an argument, it was always my fault, and she would berate me about it."
–Doug

Getting narcissists to own up to their behaviors is like trying to hold water in your bare hands—impossible, futile, and ineffective. To narcissists, nothing is ever their fault, they never did anything wrong, and they shouldn't be held accountable for their actions.

This is a major reason why relationships with narcissists can't go much deeper than surface-level. Because for meaningful relationships to grow, both people need to be honest, respectful, kind, self-reflective, and humble enough to admit their strengths and weaknesses. But in a narcissistic relationship, only one person is willing to do that (and it's not the narcissist).

When narcissists look in life's proverbial mirror, they see no one staring back at them. They don't see their reflection because they don't self-reflect. Because of this, they never see the effects their behaviors have on others. They only see other people's reactions to them.

For example, if a narcissist cheats on you, and you become angry and upset, they only see *your* actions and emotions, not what *they* did to provoke that reaction. That's why narcissists can gaslight, blame-shift, and criticize you *regardless* of what they do.

Because narcissists refuse to take their actions into consideration, they're left with no one to blame for their problems, issues, and difficulties … but *you*. In their eyes, if you have a problem with the way they're treating you—that's *your* problem. When you try to discuss their inconsistent behaviors, disrespectful and condescending tone, or flighty and questionable actions, they say the problem is that you're making it a problem.

In a narcissist's mind, if you would simply accept the lies, cheating, manipulation, and utter disregard for your feelings, then everything would be fine. This, of course, is crazy making at its finest.

NARCISSISTIC PURPOSES OF BLAME-SHIFTING

Blame-shifting is very emotionally destabilizing. No meaningful progress can be made in a conversation in which one person refuses to acknowledge their actions, emotions, and thoughts.

When narcissists blame-shift, it takes the focus off the real purpose of the conversation and puts it on the breakdown of the shared reality. Although you should be discussing the issue at hand, you're arguing about what's even real, trying to convince the narcissist why their behavior is relevant, what was actually said, and why you have a right to feel the way you do.

Because this is a futile and pointless endeavor, you spend the whole conversation attempting to bring the narcissist back to reality—a reality they are never going to admit to seeing.

This usually continues until you become so exhausted, confused, and frustrated that you stop trying to explain yourself and drop the issue altogether. In this way, narcissists successfully control the conversation, never take personal responsibility, and avoid owning up to any of their faults.

Consistent and repetitive blame-shifting is so exhausting it lessens the likelihood of you bringing up issues in the future since you learn that you never get anywhere productive. This is a poignant example of how narcissists influence you to feel helpless, hopeless, and powerless.

PASSIVE-AGGRESSIVENESS: THE UNSEEN ABUSE

"Every time I would struggle mentally, or with my self-esteem, he would blame it on something when all along it was him devaluing me. Withholding attention and affection, subtly expressing dislike of something I do, something I wear, my looks, my body, my weight. He constantly criticized my parenting decisions and beliefs and made me feel like a failure as a parent. He made me feel like nothing could please him; nothing I wanted or felt mattered. He would say things like, 'Don't gain too much weight or I won't want to be with you,' then, when I lost weight, he would say I lost too much weight, and now he's not attracted to me anymore. He would constantly 'forget' to reimburse me for shared expenses and make me feel like I was nickel and diming him when I would get upset at him for not paying for things he was supposed to."

–Jen

Passive-aggressiveness includes harmful, hurtful, or aggressive behaviors that appear in sneaky or subtle ways. These are the comments and questions that sound completely innocent or maybe even complimentary, but something in your gut tells you they're far from harmless.

Passive-aggressiveness is different from overt abuse because it's not something you can easily define as abusive. For example, people are quick to label a black eye as abusive, no matter how it happened (i.e., whether you were punched, kicked, had something thrown at you, etc.). However, people are more likely to overlook, dismiss, or completely disregard passive-aggressive comments if they don't understand the history or context of the relationship.

For this reason, narcissists often use passive-aggressive comments in public since it's a way to belittle and control you without *looking* like they're doing anything abusive. They do things like publicly voice their concerns for your mental health, even though they know nothing is wrong, or stay silent during a family conflict, even though they previously said they would support you. They'll use sarcasm, cruel humor, and being brutally "honest" to undermine you, all under the guise of a joke or of being a straightforward person.

For instance, let's say you've been working a lot of extra hours because of a big project. Although your narcissistic spouse knows this, they agree with your family when your parents criticize you for not calling them as much.

During this conversation, the narcissist looks completely innocent, even concerned for your well-being. If you call them out during this conversation, you would likely be labeled difficult, defensive, or rude. The narcissist knows this and uses people's perceptions and lack of knowledge to make you look bad.

Narcissists also display passive-aggressiveness through what they *don't* do. They "forget" your birthday or special occasion and show up late to events that are important to you. They claim to not notice that you bought a new dress, cut your hair, used a new perfume or cologne, or cooked their favorite meal.

They act upset, sad, or offended but refuse to talk about why. When you're disappointed because you didn't get the promotion, they say your current job is probably more suited for you and chastise you for being ungrateful.

At the heart of passive-aggressive comments is a sinister attempt to make you feel inferior, less than, and not enough. It's seeped in all the ways narcissists say, *"I don't like you,"* with or without words. Calling out a narcissist for being passive-aggressive is like trying to catch the wind: you know it's there, but you can't grasp it … even though you can certainly feel it.

NARCISSISTIC PURPOSES OF PASSIVE-AGGRESSIVENESS

Passive-aggressiveness fulfills many goals in the narcissist's playbook. For starters, passive-aggressiveness is a form of entitlement. Narcissists feel special when they act in passive-aggressive ways because they believe they can and should be able to act in whatever way they want.

Passive-aggressiveness allows narcissists to maintain their positive image while secretly devaluing someone. Narcissists will disguise their passive-aggressive comments as misunderstandings, claiming that the other person took what they said the wrong way or heard it out of context.

At any given moment, narcissists need someone to admire them and someone to be their emotional punching bag. Being passive-aggressive means narcissists can do both simultaneously since most people outside of the relationship don't recognize what the narcissist is doing as abusive or harmful. This means no matter where they are, they can save face and harm you at the same time.

CONTEMPT: A QUICK FIX TO FEEL "BETTER THAN"

"As soon as we were married, I noticed how critical he was of everyone around him. We couldn't even watch TV without him criticizing people's physical appearances. This also carried over to me, and I soon felt very inadequate and insecure. I couldn't cook, clean, or even do my hair without being criticized. If I got upset about something, I was told I was overly sensitive, and he would invalidate and gaslight my feelings. I was made to feel like I was the problem. I went to therapy for depression and anxiety and ended up being medicated for the first time in my life. I became isolated from family and felt emotionally deceived. I put on weight rapidly and even changed my hair color because I was sick of feeling like I wasn't good enough."
–Kate

If the world were made of narcissists, entitlement would fill the skies, and contempt would be the air you breathe.

Contempt[6] is a strong dislike, disapproval, disgust, or disdain for something or someone. In a healthy context, contempt can be felt toward things like abuse, genocide, or heinous crimes. However, for narcissists, feeling and expressing contempt is a way of life.

Narcissists hold contempt for the beliefs, values, or behaviors that impede their ability to do what they want, when they want, how they want. Principles like honesty, integrity, faithfulness, and trust, which are at the foundation of healthy relationships, are in stark contrast to narcissists' deceitful, impulsive, and egotistical behaviors.

They hate your punctuality because it highlights their tardiness. They hate your dependability because it reveals their inconsistencies. They hate your honesty because it contradicts their lies. They hate your authenticity because it jeopardizes their false image. They hate your boundaries because it blocks their ability to manipulate you.

This is why they diminish your achievements (e.g., "Anyone could do that."), make fun of your emotions (e.g., "You're so sensitive."), and disregard your requests (e.g., "Nothing is ever good enough for you."). For narcissists, contempt keeps them in control. They say things like, "You couldn't even figure that out?" "Are you seriously that desperate?" or "What kind of person would think/say/do that?"

Kelli describes her experiences:

> *"He laughs at things that are important to me. He talks bad about other women, who are similar to me, says very hurtful and belittling things as a joke, then gets mad because I can't take a joke. He makes fun of my profession, my friends, and peers. He constantly tells me that he would handle things better than me if he were me."*

Audrey shares her experiences with a narcissistic ex:

> *"He would say I was stupid; I did nothing right. When I would cry, he would say, 'you're such a baby, always crying.' He would kick me out of his house. If I found out about him cheating, he would say, 'you deserve it.'"*

All the positive things you do to make yourself stronger and healthier—like setting boundaries, trusting your intuition, and standing firm in your values—enrages narcissists because it obstructs their entitled, selfish behaviors. The better you get at setting boundaries, the less they can use you for narcissistic supply. The more you trust your intuition, the less they can effectively gaslight you. The stronger you get in your values, the less weight their manipulative words carry.

You become like a proverbial mirror, reflecting decency, patience, and kindness. But narcissists aren't those things, which is why they don't like looking into that mirror (i.e., who you are and what you stand for).

Narcissistic contempt also comes out when narcissists completely disregard or purposefully dismiss or undermine anything that is important, special, or valuable to you.

This can range from relatively small things, like asking them to walk beside you instead of ahead of you, to big-ticket items, like showing up on time to your beloved sister's wedding. Additional examples include:

- Carelessly throwing around boxes filled with sentimental items.

- Purposefully seeking out attractive business prospects even though you just caught them cheating a second time.

- Keeping old love letters from their exes even though they have a history of acting inappropriately with former partners.

- Intentionally leaving the house a mess even though they know you're hosting an important business event that evening.

- Condemning your hobbies and interests as a waste of time or pointless.

- Consistently making disparaging comments about your religious beliefs.

Understanding the reasons behind narcissists' contemptuous looks, words, and actions is essential to your healing because, without it, many people end up feeling worthless themselves as they take the narcissist's darts of disgust personally.

But remember, when narcissists experience contempt (which they do almost every day), they project that feeling onto you. Narcissists want you to be the vessel[7] that holds their self-contempt and shame, as if taking poison out of their body and giving it to you lessens their pain. But you are not a holding place for their contempt and shame. And the more you see, believe, and feel that, the less power narcissists have over you.

NARCISSISTIC PURPOSES OF CONTEMPT

Narcissistic contempt not only allows narcissists to lessen their self-loathing by projecting their contempt and shame onto you, but it also serves to destabilize and dismantle your self-esteem and self-trust. As narcissists continually treat you with contempt, you begin to absorb their self-hatred.

Contempt is part of what drives narcissists to pick you apart—criticizing, belittling, and downplaying anything good about you. And the worse you feel about yourself, the better the narcissist feels about him/herself.

The harder you try to make narcissists follow or respect rules, boundaries, or ethics, the more embittered toward you they become. The more you try to convince them that honesty and loyalty are essential to making a relationship work, the more defiant and resistant they are. This is a battle you can't win because you two don't share the same basic values or moral principles.

SILENT TREATMENT: THE ULTIMATE POWER MOVE

"She loves to give the silent treatment because she knows I'm a people pleaser. As a child, I can remember her doing this and me being left so confused as to why she was ignoring me. Often times it would be because I had a differing opinion, or I wanted something that she didn't feel I should want. Anytime I didn't fit the mold that she had fashioned me to be, she would get upset."
–Anonymous

Almost nothing brings narcissists more power than giving you the silent treatment. The silent treatment[8] is an abrupt refusal to communicate with the intent to hurt, manipulate, or control the other person. Silent treatments can take many forms, ranging from refusing to communicate at all to continually evading questions or attempts to resolve or discuss issues.

A narcissistic abuse survivor shares her experiences with the silent treatment:

> *"He started name-calling and yelling, both of which triggered some deep hurts and fears, causing me to shut down. All the projected accusations led me to*

question everything. The incessant tears were so
difficult for me to control. And he'd either get mad at
me for having emotions or completely ignore me, even
as I cried myself to sleep night after night next to him
in my own bed."

Experiencing repeated bouts of the silent treatment can be excruciatingly painful, as it feels like you're being emotionally strangled to death. They are anxiety-provoking, panic-inducing, and mind-numbingly paralyzing.

When narcissists finally break their silence, you're often so relieved that you don't bring up anything that might induce another silent treatment. This means you work harder and harder to avoid triggering topics (which means you avoid talking about things of substance or importance) to keep the peace. This is how you become increasingly disconnected from yourself, learn to expect less and less, and fall deeper into the narcissist's distorted reality.

NARCISSISTIC PURPOSES OF THE SILENT TREATMENT

In narcissistic relationships, there's a reason your behaviors and reactions feel conditioned, as if you've been programmed to respond in certain ways. There's a reason you stay quiet even when you would normally speak, ignore your needs even when you want them to be heard, and work diligently to make the narcissist happy. And that's because narcissists *are* conditioning your responses, even without saying a word.

The silent treatment is an example of behavior modification[9] where consequences are given to increase or decrease the likelihood of certain behaviors. The silent treatment *decreases* the likelihood of you asking for support, sharing your needs, or setting a boundary. Over time, you learn that pointing out the narcissist's inconsistencies, sharing your needs, asking for empathy, or making simple requests is going to be painful. So, you're conditioned to stop asking for anything.

When someone refuses to communicate with you, it *hurts*. That's because the same part of the brain that is activated when you're physically in pain is the same part of the brain that is activated when you're emotionally in pain.[10] There's a reason we say hurtful words "cut like a knife" or feel like "daggers to the chest." Words might not leave physical scars, but they bruise you on the inside.

And if you get hurt for sharing your needs, it's not long before you try not to need anything at all. And this is exactly what the narcissist wants—for you to become hollow. For them, an empty vessel is easier to steer.

WITHHOLDING BEHAVIORS:
A SILENT WAY TO MAKE YOU FEEL LESS THAN

"Our intimacy dwindled down to almost nothing ... Once, when I asked her why she no longer showed me any physical affection (I don't mean sex), she started laughing out loud, stroked her hand in the air like she was petting a dog, and said over and over, 'Aww, you want pets! You want pets!' ... This was my wife, and I could not believe I was being treated this way."
–Doug

Withholding is abusive because it's about gaining power and control. Narcissists withhold anything they know you *really* want, value, or cherish. Narcissists engage in many kinds of withholding behaviors, like blocking your access to resources or money, withholding sex, affection, important information, plans, financial passwords, denying you attention or compliments, or keeping information about your shared child's needs.

They'll often withhold the very things they previously love bombed you with. For example, if they showered you with gifts and praise in the beginning of the relationship, they'll start ignoring holidays, special occasions, and important dates. If they were initially very friendly and warm, they'll make you beg for any type of affection.

If they know your love language is physical touch, they'll avoid being intimate with you. If they know you really want to be engaged by Christmas, they'll wait until next year to propose. If they know you've been exercising for months to fit into a certain dress, they'll purposefully *not* compliment you when you wear it. Withholding is a silent way to make you feel *less than* and to trigger feelings of worthlessness, disempowerment, and insignificance.

David recounts his experiences with a narcissistic spouse:

> *"I remember wondering how she could go an entire day without speaking to me. Over the years, that grew to several days, a week, several weeks, and eventually months. The year before I eventually moved out, she spoke to me once over a nine-month period."*

Withholding is an especially harmful pattern for those who have a history of being neglected, abandoned, or uncared for. If you were raised by a narcissistic parent or experienced multiple instances of being ignored, invalidated, or dismissed, withholding patterns can feel strangely comfortable, familiar, even alluring. If you believe you're *not enough*, and the narcissist treats you like you're *not enough*, then on some level, you feel like that's what you deserve. If you're used to having your needs overlooked, it doesn't feel that unfamiliar when a narcissist ignores you.

NARCISSISTIC PURPOSES OF WITHHOLDING

Withholding keeps the narcissist in charge of the relationship. It's an unspoken way of saying, "I'm in control here." It removes your attention from your intuition and refocuses it on trying to prevent the narcissist from pulling away again.

Withholding is the cold part of the hot-and-cold cycle of abuse. Narcissists idealize you, then devalue you. They praise you, then criticize you. They give you affection, then ignore you. It's this process that makes narcissistic abuse so puzzling, disturbing, and unnerving.

With a narcissist, it's imperative to understand that not all days are bad. There are ups and downs, and highs and lows. Narcissistic abuse is a never-ending carousel of *good days* and *bad days*.

You need to understand that love bombing and withholding are two sides of the same narcissistic coin—where you have one, you'll have the other. And determining which one you'll get today is as predictable as choosing heads or tails on a coin toss.

PHYSICAL ABUSE: WHEN SADISM AND
MALEVOLENCE CONVERGE

"Nothing I ever did was good enough, I never appreciated him enough, and I swear he got high from moving the goalposts as often and unpredictably as possible ... He systematically, insidiously, sadistically, and deliberately broke me—everything I once was, I was no longer. Before he left, I was staring into a black hopeless

abyss of my future as his wife ... Come to find out, his mom and aunt, who called me multiple times the week before he left, told me this is a pattern of behavior for him ... that he is the common denominator in all his 'toxic' relationships. They encouraged me to stop apologizing for things I haven't done ... They also swore they'd never admit to the conversations and warned me against contacting his exes, 'don't ever let him find out, or else...' Another abbreviated version of the most sinister experience in my life ... I was such a strong, independent, outgoing, and great person before he destroyed me. I was so afraid I'd never find myself again. I started talking to a therapist a month after he left when I could finally breathe without sobbing. She assured me I was very stable, strong, and had been through absolute terror. I have experienced profound trauma amnesia and CPTSD as a result of it all. And it is so hard to put into words. I have learned so much about him in the last few months even still that it is terrifying to learn who he really is."
—Anonymous

When narcissists engage in physical abuse, it typically comes after a pattern of escalating behaviors. For example, it's not uncommon for physically abusive narcissists to start out by engaging in behaviors like name-calling, swearing, intimidation, and spewing insults.

Behaviors like stalking, harassment, and threatening acts of violence can also be a part of the escalation phase. These threats and insults can increase to throwing objects, smashing things, punching walls, driving erratically, or being aggressive and abusive toward pets. Eventually, their behaviors become more intense and culminate in physical abuse, like hair pulling, spitting, slapping, hitting, kicking, punching, or pinching.

When narcissists become physically abusive, they commit all the typical narcissistic patterns, plus acts of physical violence. This means you experience not only the aggressive behaviors but also the criticisms, gaslighting, projection, passive-aggressiveness, and contemptuous comments.

Narcissists will blame you for their abusive actions, saying things like "You should've known better," or "You shouldn't have made me so mad." Narcissists don't take personal responsibility, even when they've been physically violent, and you have visible proof of their abuse. Although you *might* get a watered-down apology at times, this, too, will likely be shrouded in excuses, justifications, and explanations for their abusive behaviors.

It's important to note that narcissistic men and women can engage in physical violence.[11] Narcissistic women use their assumed innocent status to their advantage, pretending to be meek, submissive, and even scared of their partners when talking to others while being aggressive, domineering, and controlling behind closed doors.

NARCISSISTIC PURPOSES OF PHYSICAL ABUSE

As with any pattern of physical abuse, the purpose is to gain power and control. Abusers seek to gain significance, feelings of adequacy, and a sense of authority by punishing and controlling you through physical aggression. Narcissists have a deep fear of being insignificant, so physical abuse can be an attempt to fill this void.

Narcissists use physical abuse and threats to get what they want, like sex, resources, control of the finances, or your unquestioning support. Narcissists always need someone else to feel small, so they can feel big. By isolating, exploiting, and intimidating you, they fill their ego with delusions of grandeur and a sense of superiority.

Narcissists care more about their reputation than perhaps anything else in life. No one is more volatile than a narcissist who's lost control or feels that their image is being threatened. Some narcissists will use physical violence or threats to maintain the image of a "happy family" or "perfect father/mother." Never underestimate how far an exposed narcissist will go to retain or repair their reputation.

If you or anyone you know is under threat of physical violence or is currently being abused, please contact your nearest emergency services or use the support resources in the back of this book.

SMEAR CAMPAIGN: CONTROLLING YOU BY CONTROLLING PEOPLE'S PERCEPTIONS OF YOU

"A week later, this friend had belittled me and then fully discarded me. I didn't even know what narcissism was at the time. But I realized she was in some kind of relationship with my husband, and then the smear campaign started. She called the therapist, who is also my younger son's therapist, and later a psychiatrist my older son saw ... the story was that I was bipolar, and she was concerned for my children. She followed me and accosted me in town about five months later ... During a custody exchange, I was parked in the open lot, waiting for my sons to come out. She came outside and threatened/harassed me, said I couldn't park there, said she'd call the police, and she did ... I moved far away; she is one of the reasons why I did so."
–Laurel

Smear campaigns have one overarching goal: to ruin your credibility, believability, and reputation, particularly amongst those closest to you. Smear campaigns can happen during and after a narcissistic relationship.

Narcissists will make a list of people to contact, telling each of them a slightly different story about the "cruel" things you've done. They take every action, word, text message, or video out of context as proof that they're telling the truth. They join organizations you're a part of, churches you attend, and causes you volunteer for to sow seeds of doubt in people's minds about who you are.

Smear campaigns are most effective when narcissists maintain good reputations themselves or remain hidden in the background. Staying as a neutral third party or not being seen at all is especially important if the smear campaign is going on while you're still together. In these cases, think of the narcissist like a ghost, going from room to room, knocking things off the walls. Even though you can't *see* them, they're still doing damage.

During a smear campaign, narcissists put a toxic twist on your personality traits or behaviors to negatively influence people's perceptions of you. For example, an extroverted spouse is mislabeled as loud and attention-seeking. An agreeable partner is depicted as being spineless and weak. A conscientious person is characterized as being controlling and oppressive. A hard-working colleague is painted as being greedy and selfish. A boundary-setting friend is portrayed as being cold and uncaring.

Kelli shares her experiences with a smear campaign:

> *"When I have tried to leave in the past—and it's been many times—he has called colleagues of mine and started arguments with them for 'my sake,' meaning he tells them that it's actually ME who has the problem with them. He threatens to tell my children bad things about me. He tells me no one else will ever love me."*

Narcissists also use society's pre-existing assumptions and biases to run a successful smear campaign. For example, narcissistic women will routinely claim that their male partner is controlling, jealous, domineering, or uncooperative since males are more likely to be viewed as assertive, unemotional, and egotistical.

Narcissistic women might also use cultural assumptions about a male's sex drive to gain people's sympathy. For instance, narcissistic women might claim that their male partner was a sex addict or "always" pushing them to be intimate, even if she was withholding sex for months or years at a time, as a control tactic.

Narcissistic men might claim their female partners are emotionally unstable, irrational, needy, or judgmental since there are gender stereotypes about women being hormonal, moody, and sensitive. Narcissistic men who are unfaithful might try to excuse or justify their infidelity by claiming that their wives refused to be intimate with them or didn't satisfy them.

Whatever the narrative, narcissists use smear campaigns to save face, justify their indiscretions, and paint a completely distorted picture of reality.

NARCISSISTIC PURPOSES OF A SMEAR CAMPAIGN

Smear campaigns serve many purposes for narcissists. At its most basic level, smear campaigns are about maintaining the narcissist's image. They want to look good while making you look bad.

But smear campaigns are so much more complex than narcissists simply telling lies about you. While in the throes of a smear campaign, you see all kinds of narcissistically abusive patterns, like triangulation, passive-aggressiveness, denial, isolation, threats, gaslighting, blame-shifting, manipulation, and criticisms. Essentially, every layer of narcissistic abuse could be understood by breaking apart the smear campaign.

Narcissists use smear campaigns because they feel *entitled* to *lie*, *distort*, *manipulate*, and *twist the truth* to their advantage. They feel a *sense of superiority* while bad-mouthing you to others as if they're above or better than all the "terrible things" you did to them.

Smear campaigns display narcissists' ongoing *contempt* for who you are and what you stand for. It's a way they gain *narcissistic supply* by gaining people's approval. They feel *special* and *validated* when they get to share their version of reality. Smear campaigns make narcissists feel *in control* and *powerful*, as they manipulate people's perceptions of who you are and what happened in the relationship.

Narcissists are notoriously *impulsive*, so gossiping and spreading rumors soothe their desire for rash action. Successful smear campaigns allow narcissists to control multiple people's reality, which is highly satisfying to their *validation-seeking ego*. Narcissists are incredibly *vindictive*, and smear campaigns offer a perfect way for them to *exact their revenge* against you for all the ways you "did them wrong."

When you dissect the multiple purposes of a smear campaign, it becomes apparent why narcissists are so fond of them. Smear campaigns are the pinnacle of narcissistic abuse, encompassing every layer of abusive patterns.

WRAPPING UP NARCISSISTS AND NARCISSISTIC ABUSE

We've covered a ton of content about narcissists—learning who they are, how they harm people, and how to recognize different types. At this point, it's time to switch gears. Part two is all about finding yourself—learning how to listen to your intuition, cut toxic ties, meet your needs in healthy ways, and set guilt-free boundaries.

PART TWO

FINDING YOURSELF

CHAPTER SEVEN

Am I Being Abused? How Your Body Warns You of Toxic Relationships

"The relationship affected my central nervous system, which was in a constant freeze and flight state, and never in a calm, relaxed state. It affected my sleep patterns, my cognitive performance and functioning, my joy for life, and mental health. I was always in search of feeling loved, respected, and understood/seen for who I was. I was unhappy, confused, doubtful, and insecure. I never felt understood and was criticized for how I thought, what I wanted to do, and how I envisioned life."
–Anonymous

Learning to recognize the early warning signs of a toxic person is all about tuning into your body—your thoughts, feelings, behaviors, moods, and nervous system responses. Trusting yourself and your intuition is critical to becoming a narcissist-resistant person because the more you trust yourself, the less susceptible you are to toxic people.

This chapter explores cognitive, emotional, behavioral, and physiological warning signs of unsafe relationships. Please keep in mind that some toxic relationships don't have blatant red flags. You are never responsible for someone else's poor or abusive treatment of you, regardless of whether you felt like something was "off" or not.

The warning signs below are meant to help you be more mindful of your body and to validate the emotional and psychological experiences that commonly occur for survivors of narcissistic relationships.

Here's a visual overview of the warning signs:

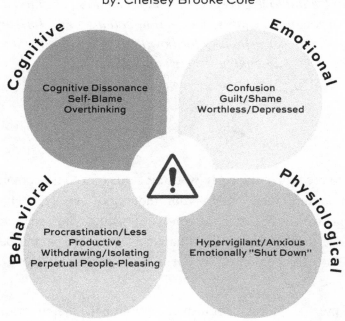

WARNING SIGNS OF NARCISSISTIC ABUSE
by: Chelsey Brooke Cole

Cognitive
Cognitive Dissonance
Self-Blame
Overthinking

Emotional
Confusion
Guilt/Shame
Worthless/Depressed

Behavioral
Procrastination/Less Productive
Withdrawing/Isolating
Perpetual People-Pleasing

Physiological
Hypervigilant/Anxious
Emotionally "Shut Down"

COGNITIVE WARNING SIGNS

The first red flag you're usually consciously aware of is changes in your thinking. In many cultures, there's a big emphasis placed on being logical, practical, and rational. You're expected to act in ways that "make sense" to avoid being illogical, silly, or foolish. Naturally, this means that when you find yourself in a relationship with someone whose behaviors *don't* make sense, you would have not only an internal desire but also a *cultural expectation* to rationalize these irrational behaviors. You think, *"It would be silly of me to end this relationship when I can't even explain what's really wrong with it."* But, in truth, the fact that someone's behaviors don't make sense *is* a red flag.

Warning Sign #1: Cognitive Dissonance

"Over time, you start to question yourself and to believe that you are the cause of the issues or the perpetrator of what they claim."
–Evie

As humans, we have an innate desire for our behaviors, thoughts, emotions, and values to align. For example, when you're married, you expect to rely on, communicate with, and receive love from your spouse. When you're married, *and* your spouse is dishonest, disloyal, and unkind, you feel uneasy and uncomfortable with that disparity. The anxiety that arises from the mismatch between your expectations and reality is called *cognitive dissonance.*[1]

Because cognitive dissonance is an uncomfortable experience, you want to alleviate those anxious feelings and racing thoughts. So, you start justifying, explaining, and rationalizing your partner's behaviors to make them fit what you expect a marriage to be. Instead of saying to yourself, *"I'm married to someone, **and** they're abusive,"* you might say something like, *"I'm married to someone who's critical of me, **but** they don't really mean it."* Some common statements you make when rationalizing and justifying toxic behaviors include:

- "Everyone says things they don't mean when they're mad."
- "She has a bad temper, but only because she had a really difficult childhood."
- "He only says that because he loves me so much."
- "I'm sure things will get better with time."
- "We've only been together two months, so he didn't know that would hurt my feelings."
- "She just needs to get away from her family, then she'll grow up."
- "He's really mean sometimes, but he always makes up for it."
- "He said it would never happen again."
- "I know she means well."
- "Everyone has relationship issues."
- "Marriage is hard work."
- "I can't expect him/her to be perfect."
- "All relationships have their ups and downs."
- "Love means you never give up."
- "It's just a communication issue."

Rationalizations and justifications also happen when you cover up, explain away, or make excuses for someone's bad behaviors. Perhaps a friend notices your partner being critical of you, so you quickly say something like, "Oh, he's just joking," or "He/she didn't mean it that way." Maybe a family member asks how you and your spouse have been, so you tell them about the handful of good days to paint the picture of a happy family.

Kisha shares her experiences with cognitive dissonance:

> *"I would second guess my intuition and would accept his truth as my own to not rock the boat. I adopted a lot of avoidance behavior ... because I didn't want to upset him or have him disappear for any amount of time. I became desperate for his validation, 'love,' attention, affection, and acceptance. I started pretending to my family and friends that things were wonderful. Everyone saw him through the lens I presented, and as the person he showed up as to them, which was very different than the actual person I was in a relationship with every day."*

When you consistently cover up your partner's bad behaviors, you isolate yourself further and further from the truth. When people don't know about your partner's criticisms, put-downs, betrayals, and lies, it's easier for you to act like they don't exist. Repeated cover-ups lead you to not even know what's real anymore. Essentially, you're gaslighting yourself.

If you find yourself consistently explaining or rationalizing someone's behaviors to stay in the relationship, there's a problem. You shouldn't have to work that hard to make someone's behaviors *make sense*.

Take a moment to think about someone you *really trust*—a person that has your back, listens to you, and understands you. Do you have to reassure yourself that this person cares about you? Do you ever feel anxious, hypervigilant, or like you're walking on eggshells around this person? If this person is healthy, you can answer "No" without hesitation. Healthy people make sense. Toxic people always keep you guessing.

Warning Sign #2: Self-Blame

"I blamed myself and made excuses for him and didn't believe he was actually the problem until very recently. I am usually a fairly happy person, and I went into a deep depression for several years."
–Heather

While some people engage in self-blame regardless of their relationship status, being with a narcissist can make even the most confident person seriously question themselves. Narcissists take no responsibility, so they search for someone who's willing to take *all* the responsibility.

Partners of narcissists tend to be empathetic, reflective, growth-oriented people who seek improvement, recognize opportunities for growth, and commit to personal development. Narcissists exploit these traits by taking your willingness to self-reflect and reframing it as proof that *you* are the one with the problem.

For example, after disagreements, you likely reflect on what was said and apologize for misunderstandings. Out of a desire to be humble and seek resolution, you say things like, "I realize what I said could've been hurtful. I'm sorry, and I want to make this work." You expect this will de-escalate the tension, they will take some responsibility as well, and the conflict will be settled.

Instead, you get criticized and gaslighted as the narcissist blames you for being purposefully vindictive, claims that you're making excuses, and asserts that the relationship will never work if you keep being controlling and manipulative.

This mix of blame-shifting, projection, abandonment threats, and gaslighting leaves you feeling deflated, discouraged, and defeated. Many people start to question their ability to solve *any* problem, even those outside of the relationship.

While self-blame can often be recognized as the anxious, guilt-ridden, frustrated feeling that surfaces during conversations with the narcissist, it can also be seen in your self-talk. Self-blame can sound like:

- "I should be grateful for what I have. I ask for too much."

- "I knew I shouldn't have brought this up right now."

- "Why can't I ever say anything right?"

- "They're doing the best they can. It's selfish of me to want more."

- "I know they left because I wasn't good enough. I should've done more."

- "I didn't explain it right; that's why they're so angry at me."

- "I can't believe I let this happen."

- "I should've known better."

- "How could I be so stupid?"

The most notable aspect of self-blame is that it always assumes you can control more than you actually can. Self-blame's voice says, *"You're responsible for everything,"* and assumes that since you're responsible, you're also to blame.

However, you can't control someone else's choices. Allow them to take responsibility for their actions like you take responsibility for yours.

Sometimes you hold onto self-blame as your last hope to make things better. After all, if things really are your fault, then *you* can fix them. Accepting that everything is *not* your fault can create a sense of hopelessness since part of you knows that if *you* can't fix it, then it won't be fixed.

Warning Sign #3: Overthinking

"I started to question myself, wondering if I was good enough or doing the right things. I wasn't making choices for myself; I was making decisions based off what I thought would make him the happiest. I didn't want to make him mad, and I didn't want to disappoint him. I found myself caring for him rather than him caring for me. I became extremely self-critical and indecisive."
–Haley

If there's one thing narcissistic abuse leads you to do—it's overthinking. From the very beginning, narcissists are selling a false story. They aren't who they say they are, they don't want what they say they want, and they don't do what they say they'll do.

But of course, you don't know this until after you've bought into the façade. It's like unknowingly stepping into a tornado and wondering why you're being thrown around. It's not until you step out of the chaos that you can accurately identify it as a tornado; then everything makes sense.

Because of this false beginning, you start overthinking very early on in the relationship. Your brain lives on a treadmill, running through every conversation and interaction, everything said and unsaid, every subtle nonverbal gesture and off-handed comment. You wonder if they meant what they said or if they were implying something else. You doubt whether you interpreted their actions correctly. You ponder whether you're making a bigger deal of things than you should. You ruminate about past disagreements and unresolved issues.

This constant overthinking leaves you with little mental energy for anything else, so you start having trouble remembering what someone just said, organizing the papers on your desk, or planning for tomorrow's tasks. You forget things at the grocery store, drive right past the place you were going, and drop the ball on calling your friend back. You can't decide what you want for dinner, which brand of cereal you should buy, or whether you should wear the black shirt or the red one. Your mind feels foggy, unclear, and slow, as if your thoughts are stuck in the mud. You can't seem to make any decisions, even small or relatively insignificant ones.

Overthinking is a big reason you start to feel like you're "losing it" or "going crazy." Since you overthink things outside of the relationship, too, you decide, *"Well, it must be me because I have trouble making decisions even when my partner isn't around."*

But that's like blaming yourself for suffocating when you're in a room that's being drained of oxygen. You wouldn't blame your body for bruising if someone else hit you, so you can't blame your cloudy thoughts on something being wrong with you.

If you haven't yet realized that you're in a narcissistic relationship, it's easy to conclude that there must be something wrong with you. And without an accurate explanation (i.e., overthinking is an effect of being narcissistically abused), you're more likely to accept the narcissist's accusations that you're difficult, judgmental, hypersensitive, or obsessed with control.

EMOTION-BASED WARNING SIGNS

Abusive behaviors reveal themselves as patterns over time, so recognizing narcissistic abuse is a process. However, one of the quickest ways to identify toxic behaviors is to notice *how you feel*. Your emotions are a feedback system, letting you know when you feel happy and secure, or anxious and confused.

You are a walking computer, your brain and body taking in more information than you can imagine, quickly processing it, and providing you signals through physical sensations that you experience as emotions. Staying mindful of your emotional states can mean the difference between *staying away from* or *getting sucked into* a narcissistic relationship.

Warning Sign #4: Confusion

"I was so deep into the manipulation at that point that I didn't even realize I was being devalued. I was so brainwashed and confused by what was going on in our relationship that I just had no idea what he was up to. I was so well played."
—Ronni

A huge sign that you're in a toxic relationship is when you leave conversations feeling more confused than when you started them. No matter how many times you replay the scenario, nothing ever adds up.

And even if you get a *glimpse* of clarity or think that you two are finally on the same page, questionable things start happening again. The same issues get recycled, the same lies get told, and the same promises get broken.

Confusion is the emotional side of the cognitive dissonance coin. While your *mind* races with thoughts—analyzing, questioning, and dissecting every part of the relationship—your *heart* is full of confusion, exhaustion, and apprehension. You try to make sense of what's happening *now* based on who you *think* they are. And you believe once you two can "figure out your differences," everything will be great. But this belief only keeps you confused. It's not until you realize they're a narcissist that you can put their behaviors in a context that makes sense.

Warning Sign #5: Guilt/Shame

"She always reminds me how useless, stupid, or lazy I am and how she has to do everything for it to get done. But when I do something, it's never done right or done well. When I would stand up for myself or try to set boundaries, she would immediately start a rage and or take things away and make threats. I feel like all my life with her has been spent trying to please her and get her what she wants."
–Anonymous

If guilt is a familiar emotion to you, this warning sign will be easy to overlook. But over time, narcissists intensify this emotion until you feel paralyzed by it. No matter what you do, it's never right or good enough. Narcissists consistently point out how harmful, ridiculous, or pathetic your personality traits, preferences, lifestyle choices, or habits are. They give you no breathing room to be *human*—any slip-up, mistake, blind error, or unintentional contradiction will be pointed out and used against you for days, months, or even years.

You feel like you can't say anything right, as if you're always offending them. You begin to internalize this and think, *"Wow! I'm always hurting his/her feelings. What's wrong with me? Am I really that inconsiderate?"* You apologize for things you didn't do, things you can't control, and things that don't even make sense.

Narcissists want you to believe that *you* are all the bad things *they* are, and guilt makes you believe you're someone that you're not. While healthy guilt can lead to positive change (e.g., you steal something, feel guilty, and stop stealing), narcissists exploit guilt for their twisted desire. Narcissists push your "guilt button" until you feel wrong for having *any* needs. To a narcissist, the fewer needs you have, the better.

Warning Sign #6: Worthless/Depressed

"I became depressed and stopped eating. I was sick to my stomach a lot, couldn't sleep, couldn't function. I just felt unwanted and unworthy and so stupid to have fallen for this pathological lying cheating narcissist."
–Christy

Many people in toxic relationships notice emotional changes that commonly occur with depression, like hopelessness, helplessness, and worthlessness.[2] Your emotions seem duller and more muted. You feel a general sense of haziness or numbness. You lose interest in things that used to bring you joy, as if the world around you is colorless. You feel drained, foggy, and sluggish. You notice changes like sleeping too much or too little, having no appetite or overeating, having no desire to take care of yourself (even general hygiene like showering), and feeling irritable without a clear reason.

Although you might be able to *identify* the things you want (e.g., being healthier, exercising more, finding a better job, managing your emotions more effectively), you keep acting in ways that are counterproductive to your goals. Self-sabotage is a way worthlessness manifests itself, as you find yourself doing things that are *logically* in opposition to what you want, but *emotionally* you feel a resistance to making better choices.

When you feel worthless, part of you doesn't think you "deserve" good things. It becomes a self-fulfilling prophecy[3]: you don't take care of yourself, so you don't think you're *worth* taking care of, which means you don't take care of yourself ... and on and on it goes. And narcissists only solidify this feeling of worthlessness by continuing to treat you like you're irrelevant.

PHYSIOLOGICAL WARNING SIGNS

"I got into this relationship at a very low point in my life, so I clung onto this relationship when my inner voice/gut was yelling to leave him. I felt myself catering to his every need and neglecting my own. I felt very angry and mentally was not in a good space."
–Valerie

Part of the reason people stay stuck in narcissistic relationships for so long is because they second-guess what they *think*. They wonder, *"Am I overthinking this? Maybe I misunderstood what they meant,"* or *"I overanalyze everything, so it's probably just me."*

But you can't overthink a gut feeling. And that's what's so powerful about physiological warning signs: they don't originate as thoughts. That jolt in your stomach, tightness in your chest, and anxious feeling in your gut happened before you even had time to think.

These body cues are due to something called *neuroception*. Neuroception is the process by which our autonomic nervous system scans the environment for cues of safety or danger.[4] While perception[5] is about the *meaning* you give to events (e.g., "I misunderstood them."), *neuroception* is about the body's *automatic response* to events. Neuroception explains why you sometimes feel tense, scared, or frozen without logically being able to explain why. You've experienced neuroception if you've ever thought something like, *"I knew something didn't add up about him/her!"* or *"My gut told me not to marry this person,"* or *"I always felt like something was off."*

Warning Sign #7: Hypervigilant/Anxious

"I was uneasy a lot. Anxious. There was so much self-blame and guilt. I always felt like I was in the wrong somehow, and at the same time felt really upset by certain 'dismissive' or 'inconsiderate' behaviors that I found to be hurtful. My mental health was slowly deteriorating, and a friend of mine recently described me as being 'a shell of a person' during the time I was with him. I just constantly felt like I was being paranoid and making up stories in my head when my doubts about him started to surface. I truly felt like I was losing my mind."
–Lena

Narcissists frequently contradict themselves and send mixed messages. You never know when a conversation will turn into an argument, something you say will be used against you, or something you do will be criticized and disparaged. When you experience repeated moments of inconsistent, threatening, and antagonistic behaviors, your sympathetic nervous system[6] (also known as the fight-or-flight response) takes over. Your brain starts actively "scanning" for possible threatening situations, and you feel the effects of cortisol (commonly referred to as the stress hormone)[7] and adrenaline. This means you live in a state of hypervigilance and anxiety.

Fight responses include things like arguing back with the narcissist, feeling intense anger, or snapping back with your own passive-aggressive comment. Those with a fight response often worry that *they* are the narcissist. However, having a strong reaction to someone else's abusive behaviors makes sense. You're trying to protect yourself, as you feel constantly attacked.

Over time, those with fight responses usually end up disengaging from the narcissist completely, shutting down, or staying constantly on edge, as if preparing for battle.

Flight responses can look like throwing yourself into work, becoming obsessed or fixated on "perfecting" a certain area of your life, incessantly worrying, or staying so busy that you don't have time to think.

The fight-or-flight response is meant to be temporary; however, in narcissistic relationships, it becomes chronic. Hoping to feel safer, you do what you can to create consistency in the chaos. You "walk on eggshells" to not upset the narcissist. You learn that when you compliment, flatter, and praise the narcissist, things are calmer, the relationship feels easier, and you feel emotionally safer.

However, when you disagree with the narcissist, ask for your needs to be met, point out inconsistencies, or try to address any issues, things become tense, the relationship feels delicate, and you feel emotionally unsafe and triggered. Slowly but surely, you become hypersensitive to the narcissist's needs, feeling like you're going to get in "trouble" if you do something they don't like.

Over time, fears generalize,[8] which means you start to feel anxious even when you see, hear, smell, taste, or touch things that remind you of the narcissist. That's why you feel panicky, sick, or on edge when you smell the perfume or cologne they wear, hear their favorite song, eat certain foods, or see things like the car they drive, the restaurant where they yelled at you, or the gift they gave you after berating you.

Remaining in this high-level state of hypervigilance has many negative effects on your health,[9] including problems with digestion, issues with muscle tension, disruptions in your sleep, weakening of your immune system, chronic pain with no medical cause, and loss of motivation. You also feel[10] more restless, agitated, and unsettled since your nervous system rarely gets to relax.

Warning Sign #8: Emotionally Shut Down

"The stuckness is REAL. I just stayed in such disbelief and delusion. I could not believe each infraction and truly started to question my own sanity. This made me incapable of change."
–Anonymous

Some people in narcissistic relationships become numb, apathetic, or shut down. While they used to feel anxious, now they zone out, as if they're mentally and emotionally unreachable.

When you're in a chronic state of stress or threat that you can't (or perceive you can't) escape from, your body moves into freeze mode. As opposed to the activating energy that comes with the fight or flight system, the freeze[11] system is focused on complete energy conservation. In this state, you feel paralyzed, overwhelmed, hopeless, helpless, trapped, depressed, dissociated, intensely self-critical, and mind-numbingly shameful.

From the shutdown state, you experience many changes in your mood, behaviors, and interactions. You become more disconnected not only from the narcissist but from people in general. You feel apathetic and heavy, so you're not motivated to seek out social support or to ask for help. You feel physically exhausted, mentally drained, foggy, and much less productive.

Because you feel as though you've *collapsed* on the inside, your body language, facial expressions, and tone of voice shifts, too. You make less eye contact, exhibit a more monotone voice, and are less emotionally expressive. This, in turn, makes feeling connected more difficult, as people struggle to understand how to emotionally reach you while you're in this detached state.

Just as with the fight or flight response, the freeze response is meant to be *temporary*. In life-threatening or extremely abusive situations, dissociating is a protective strategy. When the pain is too great, the body shuts down and checks out to protect itself.

However, feeling hypervigilant or shut down for an extended period means you feel stuck in that response. As feelings of safety and security become less frequent, you perceive that happiness, joy, and calmness are distant memories and not tangible realities.

BEHAVIORAL WARNING SIGNS

"I literally lost myself. I literally couldn't recognize myself. I had acne, anxiety, panic attacks, depression, I had no idea what was going on."
–April

When you're in a narcissistic relationship, you lose sight of *you*—the things you used to do, the goals you used to set, the places you used to go, and the person you used to be. So much of your mental, emotional, and physical energy is devoted to managing the relationship, you no longer have the emotional bandwidth to explore your values, priorities, and purpose.

Essentially, you're living in an emotional war zone. Which means a lot of your attention and energy is focused on *self-protection*. And when you're in self-protection, you don't feel *safe* to be open, engaging, and social.

And yet, many of our personal, professional, and life ambitions require us to be creative, imaginative, adaptable, expressive, resilient, dedicated, consistent, and motivated. Narcissistic relationships seep into your very being and threaten to change what you do and what you believe you can accomplish.

Warning Sign #9: Procrastination/Less Productive

"I was completely exhausted, catering to his chaos ... I thought I might be seriously ill at one point. I thought it might be cancer or something because I didn't have any strength at all ... I realize now that the only thing wrong with me was the fact that I was being emotionally abused on a daily basis."
–Miss B.

Narcissistic relationships are exhausting because you're either dealing with a conflict, preparing for a conflict, or trying to make sense of a conflict that just happened. Most of your creative brainpower is going toward understanding the narcissist—their behavior, their words, what they said, what they didn't say, and what they meant.

With so much effort dedicated to figuring out the narcissist, you're left with very little energy to plan, create, imagine, or work toward your personal or professional goals.

Narcissists point out your flaws, make condescending jabs at your career choice, and sarcastically question whether *you* can achieve your goals. The put-downs, criticisms, and mocking remarks undermine what you believe you deserve or can accomplish. And if you don't *believe* you can achieve something, you probably won't set the goal anyway. This leads to inaction, feelings of inadequacy, worthlessness, and self-directed anger for not following through, which leads to more self-doubt and procrastination.

Warning Sign #10: Withdrawing/Isolating

"His devaluing was more of a way of making me believe I was scared of life and kept me isolated, and I couldn't even go anywhere or see people. That's where he liked me, totally incapacitated. And considering I'm very outgoing, this was so hard for me."
–Yvonne

Isolation happens in almost every narcissistic relationship. You isolate because you feel ashamed about your relationship and unsure of how to explain what you're experiencing. You isolate because it's too disheartening to hear other people talk about their kind, considerate, loving partner when you know your partner is critical, argumentative, and cold. You isolate because the narcissist creates a conflict every time you make plans or visit someone, so it's just not worth the fight.

For example, narcissists criticize your friends, making up stories about how your friends don't really like you or are just using you. This plants seeds of doubt in your mind about who you can trust, which influences you to pull back in those relationships.

Narcissists especially do this if they feel threatened by your friends' success, confidence, or values. The more the narcissist believes that your friends will see through them, call them out, or try to convince you to leave, the more the narcissist will undermine those friendships.

Narcissists isolate you by controlling your time. Whether they made a rash decision to buy a more expensive car which put you in a financial bind, failed to give you enough prep time for an important meeting, or lost the documentation you needed to fly internationally on the way to the airport, you end up running from one problem to the next.

Interrupting your routine, being chronically late, and ignoring your boundaries around schedules are also ways narcissists control you and therefore isolate you from important relationships, meaningful ambitions, and personal goals.

Not only do you tend to withdraw from *others*, but you also withdraw from *yourself*. You stop doing the things that make you, *you*—like your weekly dance class, monthly dinner with friends, involvement with your church's youth group, or dedication to self-improvement. You become someone else because the narcissist has criticized or made fun of everything else you do. Toxic relationships drain you of your individuality, independence, and autonomy.

Warning Sign #11: Perpetual People-Pleasing

"I began to over-please her in a very unhealthy way. It gave me a momentary mental high. When she was happy in the moment because of something I did for her, that made me happy in the moment. Then I was constantly worried that I wasn't doing enough. I was constantly walking on eggshells around her, and I was intimidated by her."
–Doug

Patterns of people-pleasing can certainly exist prior to a narcissistic relationship. However, these patterns become intensified in narcissistic relationships. Narcissists hate boundaries, so finding someone who's willing to sacrifice their needs for others is a win in the narcissist's mind.

Narcissists *incentivize* people-pleasing as if it's an investment for your own good because, in their mind, the less you need, the better. Narcissists reward you for *not* communicating your needs. They're happier and more pleasant when you *don't* share about your wins for the day. They're less argumentative when you *don't* state an opinion that's different than theirs. They're less antagonistic when you *don't* point out how inconsistent they've been lately.

People-pleasing patterns can be a trauma response or survival mechanism.[12] Much like how fight, flight, and freeze are adaptive strategies intended to keep you safe, the *fawn* response also exists to ensure your safety by urging you to make peace, meet everyone's expectations, and dismiss or defer your own needs.

The fawn response explains how people-pleasing can become an automatic reflex, where you jump to soothe, pacify, or appease others before you've even had time to process what you're doing or why. This is especially true for those who developed fawn responses in childhood.

Chronic people-pleasing disconnects you from what's best for you. You develop a mindset that's focused on others' needs regardless of your own. You feel like you must choose between others' needs or your needs as if it can't be both.

On top of that, narcissists perpetuate this false belief by never being satisfied, calling you selfish whenever you ask for something, and acting like anything you want is a huge deal.

Statements commonly said by those living in a fawn response include:

- "I'm sorry!"

- "I always mess things up."
- "I'm so stupid; I can't believe I did that!"
- "I'm such a screwed-up person."
- "I can't do anything right!"
- "It's my fault!"

Feelings of guilt and shame are common in the fawn response since you only feel safe to move *out* of the fawn response when the people around you are happy, content, and calm.

But nothing is ever enough for a narcissist, so there are *always* more rules to follow, more expectations to meet, and more apologies to be made. And if you're waiting for a narcissist to be self-regulated before you can relax … you're going to be holding your breath *indefinitely*.

WRAPPING UP BODY-BASED WARNING SIGNS

Narcissists abuse you so subtly that you think the insecurities you're experiencing are "you" instead of "what's happening" to you. Learning to recognize these warning signs will help you be more perceptive and trusting of your intuition, as well as less judgmental toward your emotions and thoughts.

But what if you know the body-based changes you're experiencing are because of the narcissist—but you feel paralyzed to do anything about it? Or what if you're still confused, unsure if it's you, them, or a combination of both? In these instances, you might be experiencing a trauma bond, which is exactly what we'll be exploring next.

CHAPTER EIGHT

The Binding Nature of Narcissistic Relationships: Demystifying the Trauma Bond

"I felt he had this 'hold' over me and obsessively looked out for any message, text, or anything from him. The moment he messaged me, I would drop what I was doing to read his message; nothing else mattered as much as getting a message from him. My whole world revolved around him."
–Claire

There's nothing *simple* about leaving a narcissistic relationship. Hope that it'll get better, fear the narcissist will change for the next person, and guilt about not being good enough are all reasons people stay. And in some cases, due to finances, children's needs, or other life circumstances, people *choose* to stay. Everyone has a right to make their own choice, as this isn't a one size fits all decision.

However, sometimes you feel like you can't leave, even though you *want* to leave. You feel as if there's an immensely powerful, invisible force keeping you in the relationship. You think to yourself, "*I know I should leave, but I just can't. It's like I don't know who I am anymore. I'm acting in ways that aren't even me.*" Or you say to yourself, "*I keep leaving and going back. I feel pathetic. I mean, I know they're lying to me, but I want to believe them. I just want to get back to the way it was in the beginning.*" Or perhaps you ponder heavy thoughts like, "*I've ended relationships before—why can't I leave this one? I feel as if I'm addicted to them.*"

If you can relate, then you know exactly what a trauma bond feels like. A trauma bond[1] forms when you become attached to someone who also hurts you. Trauma bonds don't happen immediately. They take time and a series of progressive steps to form.

In a narcissistic relationship, trauma bonding is *bonding* that happens due to *trauma*. Trauma is the glue that holds the bond together. That's why when you *heal*—not only current but also past traumas—you become stronger, the bond becomes weaker, and you can break free.

Please know that a trauma bond is never your "fault." It's simply something that can happen due to the hot-and-cold cycle of narcissistic abuse. Some people are more likely to have adult trauma-bonded relationships because they grew up in chaotic or dysfunctional households. Regardless of your backstory, trauma bonds can develop—but they can also be broken.

As you'll see, the creation of a trauma bond is a process, and so is deconstructing it. First, we'll explore trauma bonds from an attachment and brain perspective to see how and why narcissistic relationships tend to feel so "sticky." Second, we'll look at how your family dynamics might've laid the groundwork for trauma-bonded relationships to feel "normal." And finally, I'll lay out the how-to steps for breaking a trauma bond.

Trauma bonds are typically experienced in one of two ways:

- You want to leave but feel stuck.

- You know something is off but feel too invested or confused to know what you should do.

Below is an explanation of how you feel in each scenario.

Scenario #1: You want to leave but feel stuck.

"I felt addicted to the abuse in a way. I always made excuses for him, like he's not well, or he had a hard life growing up. My empathy towards him and making excuses for him to a certain degree made me feel addicted."
—Yvonne

"I currently feel addicted, I have for many years. He's all that I know, and I hate him, but I want him ... I hate that I want him! I hate that I miss him!"
—Anonymous

You've seen the red flags. You've done the research. You've read the books. You *know* your partner is toxic, narcissistic, or unhealthy.

But you still stay.

You make up after the fights. You take the bait and respond to their antagonistic text messages. You check their social media accounts to see if they're talking to their ex. Half the time, you don't believe anything they say. And the other half, you're stunned at their cruel, selfish, and contemptuous behaviors.

You ruminate a lot, pondering questions like, *"Do they not see what they're doing? Are they that delusional? Don't they realize how toxic they are?"* And these questions are *just enough* to keep you thinking about your toxic partner way too much.

You've tried ending the relationship several times, but something always pulls you back. You're desperate to end this cycle but become overwhelmed with panic and fear when you think of ending the relationship. When you think about leaving, you feel:

- Tremendously lonely/alone
- Disconnected from everyone but your partner
- A deep sense of worthlessness
- Afraid of not finding anyone better
- Panicky or desperate
- Extremely anxious

The intensity of these emotions is unlike anything you've experienced before. You've never had such a hard time leaving a relationship, especially one that you know isn't good for you. You worry that you'll stay stuck like this forever.

Scenario #2: You know something is off but aren't sure what you should do.

"Somedays I want to leave and believe he has NPD, and somedays I wonder if he doesn't, and maybe I am to blame for some of this, and maybe he does care; it's hopeful wishing. Wishing he could become the man I thought he was, who I thought he could be."
–Chelsea

Some people describe their trauma bond as a "magical connection" and resonate strongly with statements like, "Love always finds a way," "If I'm not sacrificing myself, then I'm not showing enough love," or "Love means never giving up." Part of you knows your partner's behaviors are problematic, but a bigger part of you believes in your partner's potential for growth. You focus on how things could be different in the future, which helps you overlook their current toxic behaviors.

During the good times, you tell yourself that the bad times weren't so bad. And during the bad times, you cling to the good memories and hope for the good times to come. You tell yourself that the reason you're going through these difficulties is because you care about each other so much and that sometimes, "Love is pain."

You think, *"I've invested so much time and energy into this relationship. I don't want it to go to waste."* This keeps you stuck, feeling too invested to leave but unable to shake the feeling that something is wrong. Other days you wonder, *"What if I'm wrong and our relationship issues really are my fault? What if I regret leaving?"*

You're desperate to believe that things could be better. That you could get back to the way things were. You believe that if you could make them understand that what they're doing is harmful, they would change. You believe (or hope) *love can save them.* You feel as though ending the relationship would be like breaking off a part of *yourself.*

WHY DO TRAUMA BONDS FEEL INSEPARABLE?

Reason #1: Trauma Bonds Hijack Your Attachment Needs

Feeling connected is as much a part of being human as breathing.[2] We are born with a need to attach.[3] Reaching for connection is as natural as reaching for water when you're thirsty and food when you're hungry. As children, our need for attachment is directed toward parents or caregivers. As adults, it's directed toward the significant people in our lives, mainly romantic partners.

In trauma-bonded relationships, love becomes synonymous with abuse. The chaos and intensity feed into the idea that you have a "special," "intense," or "unexplainable" bond. If the person who's hurting you is also the person you've formed an attachment to, you feel stuck. You don't *want* to be hurt, but you also want to feel connected.

And that's why narcissistic relationships are a perfect setup for a trauma bond—because it's not *all bad*. The toxic climate of a narcissist means there will always be good days and bad days, like there will always be sunny days and rainy days. And because good days usually follow the bad days, you begin to feel as though being hurt is a gateway to being loved.

Reason #2: Trauma Bonds are Rewarded in the Brain

Narcissistic relationships are notoriously hot and cold, which means any day could be the next "good day." When rewards (e.g., a kind gesture, compliment, attentive nod, surprise vacation) are given randomly, it's called *intermittent reinforcement*.[4] Essentially, you don't know when the next reward will come—you just know it will come *sometime*.

From a brain perspective, more dopamine[5] (i.e., the "feel good" chemical) is released for an *unexpected* reward than an expected one. And the *more* dopamine that's released, the *more motivated* you are to ensure that reward happens again. For example, if the narcissist gives you *more attention* (i.e., rewards you with emotional support), the *less* you share your feelings, you're *literally* chemically motivated to share your feelings and needs *less* often.

In narcissistic relationships, you're constantly in a state of eager expectation that things will get better. Hope means you're willing to *stay longer* and *try harder,* and from a brain perspective, you're being *chemically* motivated to do so.

Not only do you receive attention and affection in unpredictable ways, but you also experience randomly dispersed bouts of rejection, invalidation, neglect, and criticism. This means you feel bad a lot, so it doesn't take much dopamine to feel *really* good. This is how you end up settling for less and less in narcissistic relationships.

When you've been deprived of decency and consistent love, you're starved for it. Narcissistic abuse creates an imbalance of dopamine by making you feel *really good* (i.e., love bombing you), then making you feel *really bad* (i.e., devaluing you), then giving you *just enough* to feel good again (i.e., hoovering you).

Realizing how the brain reinforces trauma bonds might feel discouraging at first. But consider this: intermittent reinforcement is a learning process. This means it can also be *unlearned*. Breaking the trauma bond is a process. There is a way out—keep reading, and you'll see what I mean.

Reason #3: Trauma Bonds are Strengthened by the Abuse Cycle

Trauma bonds can develop in any relationship; however, they're more likely to develop in narcissistic relationships because of the cycle of abuse.

During the love bombing phase, it's not uncommon for your new romantic interest to eclipse everything else from view. Your social life dwindles, your work takes a back seat, and your personal goals get pushed to the side. The intensity of your new romantic interest numbs and distracts you from difficulties, hurts, or disappointments you might be suffering in other areas of your life.

The initial stage of the narcissistic cycle is intense because you must feel the *highs* before you will crave the narcissist during the *lows*. Narcissists keep you coming back by giving you "everything you ever wanted" and then taking it from you, all while convincing you that if you could ever be "good enough," you could *earn* your fairytale back.

But the good times end as quickly as they began. Seemingly out of nowhere, the relationship feels much colder. Your partner becomes less attentive, more distracted, and more easily annoyed.

You wonder what happened, what you did wrong, and what changed. You begin questioning yourself, thinking perhaps you said or did something to offend your partner. Naturally, the narcissist plays right into your self-doubts, finding fault where none exist, using subtle, passive-aggressive comments to put you on edge, and gaslighting you into thinking these changes are either in your head or all your fault.

They start dropping hints about how this relationship isn't going to work. They say things like, "Maybe I should just leave since you're never happy anymore. Nothing is ever enough for you."

These abandonment threats hit you like a punch in the stomach. You take the blame and apologize for being "needy," "controlling," or "too sensitive." You stop sharing anything that might upset the narcissist. You give them reasons they should stay and list the things that make your relationship great.

Once you're in these lows, it's common to experience something called euphoric recall.[6] This happens when you start reminiscing about all the good times and fondly remembering how things used to be.

Instead of seeing the reality of what's happening, you double down on your efforts to make things work. You justify your partner's behaviors and defend the relationship. At this point, you lessen your expectations, convincing yourself that things will get better with time.

But they never do.

You experience the same relationship issues over and over. The push and pull that happens in the narcissistic cycle of abuse make these relationships *feel* addictive.

However, even though trauma bonds are described as feeling "addicted" to your partner, trauma bonds are not addictions. That's because trauma bonds are about *safety*.

You're not *addicted* to the narcissist—you're *stuck* in a pattern of safety-seeking.

The alternation between love bombing and devaluing keeps you on edge, uncertain, and emotionally fragile. You just want peace—so you do everything you can to fix or improve the relationship, which pushes you away from what's best for you and toward what the narcissist wants.

But as soon as you do one thing they want, they've changed their mind. They always find something else you're doing "wrong" or that you need to fix.

Blaming yourself for the development of a trauma bond is like blaming yourself for suffocating when you're in a room filled with poison gas. The problem isn't you—it's the environment you're in.

The narcissistic cycle of abuse keeps you spinning as your thoughts and feelings become more and more indistinguishable from the narcissist's. Intermittent reinforcement throws you off balance and disrupts the brain's reward system. And your biological need for attachment means you feel internally torn, wanting the pain to stop but feeling pulled toward the very person who's hurting you.

Understanding that there's a chemical and brain-based explanation for *why* you feel the way you do (i.e., dopamine reward system, intermittent reinforcement, and narcissistic cycle of abuse) can validate what you're experiencing.

As if that wasn't enough, some people's likelihood for developing a trauma bond happened way before their adult narcissistic relationship(s).

FOUNDATIONS FOR A TRAUMA BOND: FAMILIAR DOESN'T NECESSARILY MEAN HEALTHY

"I grew up quite stressed and possibly depressed. I remember as a young child glad to go to bed and often cried myself to sleep, but I never knew why."
–Anonymous

As a child, you don't know if how you're being treated is *healthy* or *unhealthy*. You don't even know that healthy or unhealthy exists. You just know what *is* in your household. How your parents or primary caregivers treat you sets the foundation for what you believe is *normal* in relationships.

If they were kind, consistent, respectful, attentive, and emotionally available, then you expect future relationships to mimic that model. Similarly, if your parents were inconsistent, emotionally unavailable, neglectful, withholding, or critical, then that becomes what you expect in future relationships.

Remember, we all have a basic need to attach. As a child, attaching to your caregiver fulfills a primal need for safety. It subconsciously answers the question, *"Who will take care of me?"*

Whether you have a safe or unsafe parent is irrelevant to your biologically based attachment need. As a child, deciding *not* to attach doesn't even feel like an option. So, in an effort to meet your attachment need, you seek a relationship with someone who also invalidates, neglects, and criticizes you.

When your invalidating parent is upset, you blame yourself. When they have a rare "good day," you do everything you can to keep it that way. To avoid conflict and believe you have a "happy family," you justify, rationalize, and make excuses for your parent's hurtful behaviors. Or you absorb your parent's bad treatment of you and form beliefs like, "I'm flawed," "I'm unlovable," "I'm bad," or "There's something wrong with me."

This type of parental relationship is an example of a trauma bond. But you wouldn't have called it a trauma bond; you would've called it *love*.

If behaviors like the silent treatment, yelling, and arguing, or issues like addictions, enmeshment, or abandonment were present in your family of origin, you see these things as normal, expected, or "how things are."

That's why adult narcissistic relationships that are characterized by alternating patterns of idealization and invalidation feel strangely comfortable. And that's because these patterns are *familiar*. And whatever feels *familiar* gets interpreted as *love*. "Love" becomes synonymous with however you were treated in your family of origin. And in a toxic household, love and chaos become one and the same.

As a child in a dysfunctional environment, you don't have the perspective to realize that your family members' behaviors have nothing to do with you. Instead, you internalize these issues and feel not enough, different, weird, out of place, or like you don't belong. These feelings create *core beliefs* or perspectives that shape how you view yourself, others, and the world. You end up believing things like:

- "If I say what I really need, people will leave me."

- "All men (or women) cheat and can't be trusted."

- "Most people will use you if they get the chance."

- "Marriage is hard work."

- "The only person you can really trust is yourself."

- "All relationships have their ups and downs."

- "Love means you never give up."

- "I'm not lovable as I am."

- "Other people's needs are more important than mine."

- "If I say how I really feel, people will get mad at me."

These beliefs develop because you're trying to make sense of what's happening in your household. And in a way, these beliefs might've kept you "safe" in that environment. For example, if you were criticized, scolded, or ignored for sharing your feelings, then shutting down is exactly what you needed to do to keep yourself safe.

However, now that you're an adult, continuing to believe that shutting down is "normal" or part of being a "good person" keeps you stuck. Beliefs that develop out of toxic environments keep you stuck in toxic environments.

For example, if you have an overarching belief that "everyone cheats," you live as if that's reality. So, you're not looking for someone who *won't* cheat (since that's not in your reality)—you're looking for someone you could get over if (or when) they do.

Beliefs formed while in dysfunctional environments also don't work because they're full of contradictions. Part of you wants to feel unconditionally loved, but the other part of you doubts this is possible. So, you try to "play it safe" by getting with someone who either (a) love bombs you, which you mistake for "real love," or (b) is emotionally distant, which allows you to live with one foot out the door.

If you don't process and heal your traumas or attachment wounds (i.e., emotional hurts that develop from invalidating/neglectful/harmful relationships), you're likely to keep playing out these push-and-pull patterns.

Essentially, you get caught trying to win over an unwinnable parent by winning over an unwinnable partner. Your subconscious goal is to heal—to find a way to solve past unresolved issues. However, what you end up doing is deepening the trauma wound, thereby strengthening the trauma bond.

If this is the first time you're exploring how your family of origin impacted you, or if something in the previous section hit you particularly hard, I want you to *pause* and *breathe*. Take a walk, journal what's coming up for you, call a trusted friend, or schedule a therapy session. These issues are not easy to look at, and you need to take care of yourself throughout this healing journey.

The next section on how to break a trauma bond will be here when you're ready. Don't rush yourself if you feel overwhelmed or dazed. But if you're eager to find out how to heal and break free, read on.

HOW TO BREAK A TRAUMA BOND

"I have been investing a tremendous amount of time in my self-healing in the last year. I have gained a deep and rich understanding of narcissism traits, behaviors, tips, and strategies on how to cope and respond to a narcissist and how to establish boundaries to preserve your peace and self-worth. It has been an amazing and eye-opening journey and one that I hope to keep learning and discovering and hopefully empowering and helping other people going through the same life experiences. My central

nervous system is able to respond in a calmer, more reflected state. I do not feel the urgency to quickly respond to texts/emails and have built essential boundaries for myself. 'Once you see it, you cannot unsee it!'"
–Anonymous

We make relationship choices from the unhealthy parts of us until we heal. This is why understanding narcissism is only half the equation to true healing.

Recognizing when you're being gaslighted doesn't guarantee you'll walk away. Knowing someone is a narcissist doesn't *automatically* break a trauma bond. It's an essential first move, but it's not a checkmate. However, understanding narcissism *and* healing yourself *is*.

Dismantling the trauma bond is a process, but here's what you need to understand first and foremost: you're *not* addicted to your partner. They aren't the solution. They aren't so vital to your life that you wouldn't be able to survive without them.

Narcissists make you sick while selling themself as the cure. Through gaslighting and shame-inducing comments mixed with idealizing and future faking, narcissists convince you that they are what you need. That they are your source of comfort and stability, and without them, you would be lost, lonely, and unloved. What they never tell you (and what they hope you don't figure out) is that *they* are the reason you feel so destabilized in the first place.

Trauma is the glue that holds narcissistic trauma bonds together. Breaking the trauma bond from a narcissistic relationship is about recognizing, processing, and healing past and current traumas. The process looks something like this:

- Learn about narcissism and narcissistic abuse.

- Understand the ways narcissistic abuse personally affected you.

- Reflect on why you are/were in narcissistic relationships.

- Work on healing past and current traumas, triggers, or attachment wounds.

- Develop healthy boundaries, coping strategies, and safety-seeking behaviors.

- Cultivate healthy relationships and support systems.

- Engage in post-traumatic growth strategies for ongoing healing.

These steps are not necessarily linear, and some of them may overlap (e.g., healing trauma and developing better boundaries often happens at the same time). However, these steps show you what breaking the trauma bond looks like and how it's absolutely possible!

You might notice that none of these steps include leaving the relationship. Some people may not be able to leave, and others may choose to stay.

Breaking a trauma bond isn't just about leaving the relationship. It's about breaking the bonds that hurt you. It's about knowing on a deep level that you are whole on your own. It's about learning to feel safe in your body and not seeking safety in someone else.

However, if leaving is an option, I would highly encourage you to consider it. No contact is the best option if possible.

The steps to break a trauma bond are incorporated into the structure and content of this book, including insights and practical strategies needed for change. Steps one and two were covered in earlier chapters on understanding narcissism, and steps three through seven start below and run throughout the rest of this book.

WHY ARE/WERE YOU IN A NARCISSISTIC RELATIONSHIP?

Step three of breaking the trauma bond asks you to reflect on how you came to be in a narcissistic relationship. Some people discover that this narcissistic relationship was their first truly harmful relationship. If this is you, then I encourage you to reflect on what was happening in your life at the time this relationship began.

Consider if you had any recent changes, fears, or insecurities that left you vulnerable to this type of relationship. Had you recently moved, lost a loved one, started a new job, or experienced a breakup? Were you feeling rejected, anxious about being single, uncertain about your future, or looking to settle down? Explore what you were focusing on, how you were feeling, and how the narcissist presented themself to you.

Cynthia explains the beginning of her narcissistic relationship like this:

> *"In the beginning, we were in different states (TX and AZ). He would call me and video chat every morning and every night, and throughout the day. He would tell me I was so beautiful, and he loved how strong I was for surviving narcissistic abuse and breast cancer. He said he loves me so much and would never hurt me like my exes had hurt me."*

If this was your first toxic relationship, you might realize that you simply didn't know what you didn't know, but now you can recognize narcissists from a mile away.

However, if you're like most people, you realize that you've had several toxic, narcissistic, or harmful relationships. The most addictive-feeling trauma bonds happen when your current relationship triggers unhealed core wounds.

Core wounds are emotional or psychological hurts (often with origins in childhood) that impacted you in a profound way and continue to affect your decisions, feelings, thought patterns, or behaviors. Feeling not enough, unlovable, broken, flawed, or worthless are common core wounds, as are fears of being abandoned, rejected, disowned, or unprotected.

Lola explains why she felt so trauma bonded to her ex:

> *"I grew up feeling 'not enough.' My dad was cold, distant, and emotionally unavailable. He left my mom and married his affair partner. Even though I wanted to feel 'good enough,' deep down, I feared I never would be. So, when my ex started treating me like I wasn't enough, it felt strangely familiar. As if it validated what I always thought of myself. And when he was unfaithful, I stayed. I desperately wanted to be 'normal' and have a healthy relationship. Plus, I felt sick every time I thought about leaving. After much heavy healing work, I eventually left that toxic relationship. It was the hardest thing I've ever done. But it also led to my biggest transformation. When I finally treated myself the way I wanted others to treat me—it was a turning point in my life."*

Unhealed core wounds shape your decisions in silent ways. These are the wounds that get triggered every time you try to leave this relationship (or every time the narcissist pulls away). You need to bring to light the subconscious fears that bubble to the surface when you're faced with ending this relationship or emotionally disengaging from someone who hurts you. These are the wounds you need to heal to start breaking the trauma bond.

Here are some questions to get you started:

- When you think about leaving this relationship (physically or emotionally), what emotions or sensations are you aware of?

- Have there been other relationships (particularly in your childhood) when you felt these emotions?

- What was happening in those relationships when you felt these emotions?

- What beliefs did you form about yourself due to these experiences (e.g., "I'm not worth taking care of," "No one wants me," "I'm broken and damaged," "The people I love always leave me," "I'm only as valuable as I am helpful," "Other people have more worth than me," "I'm not lovable.")?

- Are these beliefs related to your core wounds (e.g., fear of abandonment, never feeling good enough, feeling worthless or inadequate, feeling dismissed, overlooked, ignored)? How?

Journaling your answers and taking steps to heal (through therapy, coaching, personal development work, etc.) is how change happens. The more you strengthen yourself—the weaker the bonds become.

ACKNOWLEDGE THE IMPACT OF YOUR CHILDHOOD EXPERIENCES

As a child, you didn't have the luxury of seeing your home life from the outside in. You were just *in* it—living it—surviving it. Which means those core beliefs about who you are, what you deserve, and what "love" feels like were impressed upon your heart and mind before you even realized what was happening.

But no matter how far away your childhood seems, it's important to give yourself room to think and feel things *now* that you didn't feel comfortable doing as a child. As an adult, you can reflect on the way you were raised and decide, "How my parents treated me was not okay," "I never want to raise my kids like that," or "I really wasn't nurtured the way I needed to be."

Some people feel hesitant or guilty thinking or speaking "negatively" about their parents or family of origin. This is especially true if you were told by caregivers that "we did the best we could" or that "you should be grateful" because they had it worse.

But there is no appropriate time to compare hardships, as if someone else's pain means you don't have a right to feel your own. Acknowledging your childhood experiences, whether good or bad, is not about blaming or criticizing your parents. It's about giving space for your inner little girl or boy who deserves to be seen, validated, and understood.

Sharing your insights with someone is optional but not necessary. This is a highly personal journey of self-reflection and self-compassion, which means *you* get to decide who sees your transformation.

But I will say this: make sure you're protecting yourself during this process. Looking at childhood wounds can leave you feeling bare, exposed, and delicate. Don't share the raw parts of you with those who can't appreciate the beauty of vulnerability.

WRAPPING UP TRAUMA BONDS

Untangling yourself from trauma-bonded relationships takes time because they're unlike any other relationship. When you're trauma bonded to someone, you feel like you're in a deep pit that you can't get out of. And sometimes, you see the way out, but you're scared to climb out into the unknown.

This is why I encourage you to slow down and really evaluate why this relationship feels so "sticky." Narcissists use what they know about you to keep you feeling stuck.

If they know you grew up feeling unheard, rejected, overlooked, or criticized, they'll use that knowledge against you. They'll threaten to leave you, ignore your communication attempts, and tell you that anyone would feel "lucky" to be with them. These behaviors deepen the trauma bond. And if these manipulations also hit on a core wound—they strengthen the trauma bond even more.

But when you educate yourself on narcissistic abuse *and* heal your traumas, core fears, and attachment wounds, you cut some of those trauma-bonded cords. When you take steps to heal your hurts, you take your power back.

Narcissists will keep being narcissists no matter what you do. They will lie, belittle, gaslight, and manipulate to stoke that trauma-bonded fire. Narcissistic abuse conditions you to believe that meeting the narcissist's needs is necessary for your safety.

But now you know why you feel the way you do. You're not crazy, broken, or weak. Your brain and body are trying to keep you safe by urging you to stick with what feels *familiar*, and that's why you feel panicky and paralyzed when you think about leaving or disengaging. And perhaps your early experiences set the stage for the hot-and-cold cycles of narcissistic relationships to feel "normal."

But you don't need the narcissist to survive. In fact, their abuse is what's making it hard to breathe in the first place.

If you'd like my actionable step-by-step guide to breaking a trauma bond (the same process I use with my therapy and coaching clients), get it at https://www.chelseybrookecole.com/break-the-bond or scan the QR code.

Now that you understand the trauma bond, how it works, and why these relationships feel so binding, it's time to dive into your childhood and family dynamics to heal any wounds that may be keeping you stuck in unhealthy relationships.

CHAPTER NINE

Reparenting Yourself: Why Your Inner Child Still Needs You

"It's not selfish to protect your peace. It's critical to breaking the cycle."
—Anonymous

Trust is at the foundation of any good relationship. Without it, there's no substance to build on. If you can't trust someone to be consistent, honest, and loyal, then you can't trust them enough to be vulnerable, to share your deepest fears and hopes, or to be authentically you. If you can't trust someone, you can't feel safe with them. And if you can't feel safe with them, you can't develop a meaningful relationship with them.

Seeds of distrust destroy a relationship. And yet, isn't this what we do with ourselves?

We don't listen to our gut. We let our boundaries get pushed. We place our opinions below everyone else's perspectives. We settle for what's given to us instead of asking for what we really want. We don't follow through on the positive things we say we'll do for ourselves. We don't check in with our thoughts, feelings, wishes, expectations, or goals. We don't know who we are, and we don't know why.

But is it really any wonder?

If you never checked in with your friends, would you feel close to them? We schedule date nights, call loved ones, have family get-togethers, and take trips with friends to keep our connections strong. We spend time together, talk to each other, share with each other, and support each other to feel close and safe.

Not knowing who you are, what you want, or how you feel is a result of chronic disconnection. But no matter how internally divided you feel right now, you can become an authentically unified individual. Puzzles are put together one piece at a time; you can be, too.

HOW FAMILY SHAPES YOUR SELF-RELATIONSHIP

Most people are overwhelmed by the idea of getting to know themselves because they don't know where to start. But don't worry—I'll show you exactly where to begin.

Although it might sound counterintuitive at first, you make more progress in the long run by *starting slow*. If you rush this process, the outcome will feel inauthentic, fragile, and unsustainable.

You likely don't know who you are because you haven't felt free to be you. Don't be another voice that says you need to "hurry up" or "get over it." Set the tone for this journey by giving yourself the space to grow without judgment, deadlines, or expectations.

To start, take a moment to reflect on your childhood. Were you allowed to "feel your feelings?" Were emotions even discussed or acknowledged? Many people discover that they weren't taught to think about how they felt or what they needed. This is especially true if you were raised in a household without *mirroring*.

Mirroring[1] happens when you reflect others' emotions back to them. For example, if you're upset by something that happened at school, and your parents listen attentively and respond with, "Sounds like you're feeling sad about being left out," then you gain insight as to what you're experiencing and why.

This increases self-awareness of your thoughts, feelings, beliefs, needs, physical sensations, and physiological responses. You learn what happens in *your body* when you're mad, sad, frustrated, confused, anxious, jealous, lonely, afraid, and any other emotion. You learn how your thoughts create certain emotions and what you need to feel better. Essentially, you learn how to care for your mental and emotional well-being through healthy mirroring.

However, if you were raised by a narcissistic, toxic, neglectful, or otherwise preoccupied parent, then you didn't receive proper mirroring. In fact, instead of being given a mirror to get to know yourself, you were likely given a *mold* to fit into.

So, instead of looking *inside* yourself to determine what you felt, wanted, or needed, you learned to look *outside* yourself to see what was acceptable, expected, needed, or rewarded. You learned to *externalize* your sense of safety, scanning the environment for potential threats to your well-being, paying extra attention to the emotional temperature in the room, and looking for ways to please others.

You might've developed beliefs like, "I can only be okay if everyone else is okay," "My job is to meet everyone else's needs," "I can (or should) make this work," or "How I feel isn't as important as what others want from me."

But when you externalize your sense of safety and look to others to determine how you feel, you place *your north star* in someone else. This means your compass is always changing direction, depending on how others around you are feeling. You never know what you want, how you feel, or what you think.

Building a relationship with yourself is about learning to *internalize* your sense of safety so that no matter what's going on around you, you feel sure of your needs and your ability to meet them.

HOW TO BUILD A RELATIONSHIP WITH *YOU*

Even though it might not be where you want it to be, you already have a relationship with yourself. If you relate to looking for safety in others, you likely have a highly critical relationship with yourself— one where you doubt your right to feel the way you do, question your thoughts and reactions, and worry that you ask for too much.

You might struggle to differentiate between *your* thoughts and feelings and *other people's* thoughts and feelings, particularly if you're an empath or highly sensitive person. Learning to hear your voice is a process, but one you can absolutely follow with the guide below.

I want to note a couple of things before we dive into the how-to part of self-relationship building. First, healing is not a linear journey. And because of that, there is no such thing as taking a step back. Once you know something, you can't "unknow" it. You can never go back to the way you were yesterday.

So don't worry about "going backward" or "not progressing." Healing isn't something you *do* and then you're done with it. Healing is a way of life. It's a thread that weaves itself into your very being, mingling with everything you do and who you are.

Secondly, as I said in the beginning of this book, this is *your* journey. I am not the author of your story. I am simply a guiding voice that you can choose or choose not to listen to. I don't get to dictate what healing looks like for you.

Many times, we want someone to tell us what to do because we feel safer following someone else's rules. But my hope is for *you* to learn to trust *you*. There is no time limit or timeline for self-relationship building. Wherever you are and whatever you're doing ... you're right where you're supposed to be. *Trust yourself and trust this process.*

Phase #1: Listen to Yourself

Learning to hear your voice is essential because *you can't have a relationship with someone you don't know*. And by the time you reach adulthood, it's very possible that you've never given yourself the space to know *you*. In fact, you might feel like there's a lot of excavation to be done before you can find yourself. But there's a simple way to cut to the core of who you are. And it's by practicing something called *metacognition*.

Metacognition[2] is the act of thinking about your own thoughts. You engage in metacognition when you bring to *conscious* awareness the thoughts, feelings, or beliefs that normally remain in your *subconscious*.

Metacognition is a form of *mindfulness*[3] or the practice of being aware of your internal state or surroundings. You can practice metacognition by noticing and observing your thoughts and feelings instead of judging or reacting to them. Treat your thoughts like clouds. Look at them, watch them change shape, and let them pass by.

If you're just going through the motions each day, you're not aware of how you feel, what you think, and, more importantly, *why* you think, act, and feel the way you do. But this is crucial to your healing! Because we often judge what we don't understand.

For example, if you feel irritable but don't know why, you're likely to blame yourself for having a bad attitude and feel ashamed for being irritable for "no reason."

However, if you're aware that you feel irritable when you're overwhelmed, you can skip the self-blame and plan ways to decompress. Shame about how you feel adds an extra layer of emotion to process through because whatever you judge gets stuck. So, the longer you judge what you find, the longer you'll stay stuck in that emotion or belief.

It's important to recognize that *you* are not your *thoughts*. If you discover something during this process that you don't like about yourself—the way you react, how you think about a certain topic, or your feelings toward a particular person—take note and circle back to it in the next phases.

It's very important that you *don't* take this new awareness and add it to your list of "failings." Because if you do, you're perpetuating the belief that something's wrong with you and that you need to be fixed. If you jump to "fix" yourself, you will end this process feeling more broken than when you started it.

To avoid judging yourself, preface your thoughts or feelings with the statement, "I have the thought/feeling that…" and then complete the sentence.[4] This gives you the psychological flexibility to realize that a thought doesn't have to define you. You're acknowledging that there's a difference between who you are and what you think. You can have many thoughts—but who you are is defined by what you do with them.

Part of healing is letting yourself be heard, seen, and understood as the raw, unedited version of yourself. The way a parent should love a child unconditionally. Except this time, the person who is seeing and understanding you—is you!

For example, imagine you have a conversation with a colleague, and as soon as you walk away, you think to yourself, *"She probably thought what I said was so ridiculous. I should just keep my opinions to myself!"*

Without metacognition, you react to that thought as if it's *true* and continue acting in accordance with that belief by not giving your opinion next time. **With** metacognition, you're *aware* that you had a critical thought about yourself, so you *don't* automatically react as if that thought is true, which gives you the space to *choose* a different thought and action in the future.

One practical method that can help with metacognition is the acronym CALM, which stands for consider, accept, learn, and move. Here's how it works:

- Consider the thought or feeling as a visitor. Notice what you're thinking without judgment. You are not your thoughts! Having a thought doesn't make it true.

- Accept your thought or feeling as being there for a reason. Don't fight it. You give away your power when you have a strong negative emotional reaction to a thought. Nothing happened in this moment to make that thought true. Be quick to accept how you're feeling, whether you understand it or not. You're not consenting to stay in this state; you're simply acknowledging that this is the thought or feeling you're having in this moment. Humans have thoughts or feelings, so allow yourself to be human.

- Learn from this feeling or thought. Take a curious approach. Ask yourself, *"What's this thought or feeling teaching me?"* Maybe you need to give yourself more acceptance and less judgment. Maybe you feel stressed because you haven't taken a break or eaten anything all day. Ask yourself what you need instead of making a judgment about the thought or feeling.

- Move your mind and body. After you've taken a few moments to reflect, move your body. Do something that excites, motivates, soothes, or inspires you. Go for a walk, move into a new environment, do some stretches, or get a drink of water. Your mind and body are connected, so as your body moves through space, your mind moves through thoughts and feelings, too.

Reflecting instead of *reacting* is a process and one that takes practice. This is not a time to judge, analyze, or scrutinize how you feel. This phase is about noticing and observing your emotions, thoughts, triggers, beliefs, reactions, opinions, values, and general outlook on life.

Remember, *you* are getting to know *you*. When you start a relationship, you spend a lot of time listening, talking, sharing, and getting to know one another. This is exactly what you're doing with yourself. Understandably, this may feel awkward, uncomfortable, or unfamiliar at first. But it doesn't matter where you start—only that you follow through.

Phase #2: Find Your Authentic Voice

As metacognition becomes more of a habit, you'll notice certain patterns in your thoughts or feelings. For example, you might find that you feel guilty ... a lot (and for no apparent reason). You might experience waves of sadness, become overtaken with grief, frequently anticipate that someone is going to be upset with you, or feel anxious at seemingly random moments. You might find that you're incessantly critical of yourself and that your internal dialogue is filled with things you "should" be doing and "reasons" that you're not enough.

Be curious about your reactions, emotions, and automatic self-talk. Ask yourself, *"Does that voice even sound like me?"* You might find that many of your current thoughts, feelings, and reactions don't feel genuinely *you*, even if they are automatic.

For example, if your parents were critical or dismissive, you're likely to be critical and dismissive of yourself, too. That judgmental voice in your head that rises to the top and declares, *"That was stupid,"* *"No one cares what you think,"* or *"You shouldn't feel that way,"* isn't even *you*! It's the voice of your internalized critical parent.

Once you're aware of your thought patterns, consider what core beliefs they're attached to. For example, beliefs like, "If I can predict what people need, I'll be safe," "If I can meet everyone's needs, I'll be safe," or "If I can be good enough, I'll be safe," are common for survivors of narcissistic abuse. These beliefs subtly imply there is safety in self-criticism.

And interestingly enough, an inner critic is almost always a protective voice. Your inner critic believes that finding your flaws will protect you from people's judgments. So, although that inner critic might've pushed you to be an over-achiever growing up and therefore kept you "safe" from other people's judgments, it's hurting you now. Sometimes the beliefs, habits, and emotions that kept us safe in childhood only harm us in adulthood.

Right now, the thoughts that are most familiar to you are the ones you believe are "true." So, if you're familiar with being self-critical, it will be easy to believe that voice speaks the "truth."

But an inner critic can never be your authentic voice.

Why? Because you weren't born being self-critical. You didn't even know what that meant until someone taught you. Babies don't think to themselves, *"Mom and Dad are so exhausted; I'll just go hungry,"* or *"I don't deserve to be cuddled because I cried too much today."*

They have no shame in asking for their needs to be met. They don't believe they must be perfect to be loved or feel uncomfortable accepting affection. And that's not because they're selfish! It's because they haven't learned that there's anything wrong with having needs, asking for help, or being unconditionally loved (because there's not).

Phase #3: Practice Emotional Flexibility

During this process, you'll recognize that some emotions *feel* much bigger than you would expect. That's why creating high distress tolerance is essential to your healing journey. Distress tolerance[5] describes your ability to manage difficult emotions and situations.

People who have *low* distress tolerance become easily overwhelmed by stressful situations and are likely to give up when things get difficult. People with *high* distress tolerance can ride out the waves of intense emotions and stick to their goals despite the challenges.

Increasing distress tolerance is about noticing your emotions without becoming overwhelmed by them. Take a step back and explore why a particular emotion is so intense. For example, you might ask yourself, *"On a scale of 1–10, realistically, how big of a deal is this event/interaction?"* Then, ask yourself, *"On a scale of 1–10, emotionally, how big of a deal do I feel like this is?"*

Emotions that are out of proportion to the current situation likely mean that a core wound is being triggered. Core wounds are hurts that developed in childhood and relate to our deepest fears, insecurities, or vulnerabilities. Fears like being abandoned, rejected, or ignored, insecurities like not being good enough or being criticized and shamed, and vulnerabilities like not belonging, feeling left out, or being ridiculed can all be triggered when situations arise that remind you of that core wound.

An unmistakable sign that a core wound has been triggered is when suddenly, even though you're a grown adult, you feel like a kid again. You feel small, invisible, powerless, helpless, defenseless, out of control, or whatever uncomfortable emotion was most common for you as a child. In that moment, you don't even feel like your adult self is reacting to the event; instead, you feel like your inner child is the one in charge of your thoughts, feelings, and behaviors.

To help you through these triggering emotions, ask yourself these questions:

- What age does this emotion feel like? Even when we're adults, sometimes we feel like throwing a two-year-old temper tantrum or acting defiant like an angry teenager. Knowing what age this emotion feels like can help you figure out why this specific event is so triggering.

Once you've identified the age of that emotion, explore its roots:

- What was going on in your life when you were that age?
- What emotional need wasn't getting met?
- What did you need at that time to feel safe or cared for?
- What can you do now for your inner child to make him/her feel safe or cared for?

Exploring the origins of emotions is vital to your healing because you are one continuous, intertwined human being. You are not separate from the experiences, emotions, fears, or events that you went through as a child. You are not automatically healed from past wounds just because you grew in age. Unprocessed emotions get stuck, no matter how far away you are from that moment chronologically.

This makes more sense when you consider that there are many "parts"[6] that make up "you." You might resonate with having an inner child, inner critic, perfectionist, nurturer, protector, free spirit, or logical part.

We often unknowingly identify these "parts" in the way we talk, saying things like, "Well, part of me wants to do (this) but another part of me thinks (this)." Recognizing the different "parts" of you is a helpful way to understand why you sometimes feel internally stuck or conflicted.

Different parts are triggered by different emotions, and each part has its own belief about how to stay emotionally safe. For example, the perfectionist is scared that if you stop trying to be perfect, you'll get hurt. The perfectionist urges you to work relentlessly, be self-critical, and never stop achieving. If the perfectionist is unheard or unacknowledged, it will keep driving your behaviors because parts that are ignored only grow louder and bolder.

However, if you pause and acknowledge the perfectionist's efforts to keep you safe (instead of judging it), then you allow the perfectionist to breathe and rest. Unacknowledged parts or emotions get louder because they sense that you're not listening to them—perhaps you're used to dismissing your emotions since they were dismissed by others in the past. But healing means every part of you—every emotion—gets a voice.

Answering the question "Who am I?" is about allowing space for *all your parts* to be seen, heard, understood, and accepted.

Once you become familiar with your emotional triggers and various parts, you're ready to explore the question, "What do I need?"

Phase #4: Meet Your Unmet Need

How you talk *to* yourself *about* yourself is at the foundation of a healthy self-relationship. That's why things like metacognition, mindfulness, awareness of your parts, and high distress tolerance are invaluable first steps to healing.

But knowing what you're feeling is only half of the equation to healing. The other half is doing something with that awareness. Once you become aware of an emotion or need, the next step is to meet that need with compassion. It might take some time to figure out how to do that, especially if this is the first time you're giving yourself the space to explore your own needs.

But self-compassion can be learned like any other skill. Before we explore how, ask yourself: *is it hard for me to show compassion to others?* If your answer is "not at all" (which I suspect it is), then you already have everything you need to be self-compassionate. You just need help to see it. It's like you've been holding a flashlight to your chest your whole life and thinking you have nothing to light your path. You've always had the ability; you just haven't pointed it in the right direction.

(If you were raised in an abusive or dysfunctional home and struggle to be compassionate toward others, it's likely you developed overly rigid boundaries to protect yourself. We'll cover this more in the next chapter. Either way, the steps to build self-compassion apply to you, too!)

Self-compassion[7] is made up of three elements: self-kindness, common humanity, and mindfulness. Self-kindness means you give yourself grace instead of judgment. You accept that you're not perfect and that life doesn't always go to plan—but that doesn't mean you're worthless or broken. Compassion[8] literally means "to suffer with," so self-compassion is to acknowledge, hold space for, or be with your own suffering.

Common humanity is about recognizing that everyone goes through difficulties. When you accept that things like disappointment, loss, grief, and betrayal are human experiences and not isolated incidents, you feel less alone and more connected. Common humanity helps you have self-compassion because you know you're not the only one who feels rejected, abandoned, or not good enough at times.

Mindfulness helps you create space between your thoughts or feelings and self-worth. It's the difference between *"I'm having the thought that I'm worthless"* vs. *"I'm worthless."* The first acknowledges the feeling is uncomfortable but temporary, while the latter asserts that the feeling is permanent, unchangeable, and true.

Being mindful means sitting with difficult emotions while recognizing that they can change, which helps you have more self-compassion during intensely difficult experiences.

Developing coping skills that support your ability to practice self-compassion is very important. That way, when you have a need, you already know what you can do to re-energize, refresh, and restore you. Here are some questions to journal about to get you started, dispersed with some coping strategies you can start using immediately:

Social Supports

- Who is my most trusted friend(s) or family member(s) that I can turn to for support?

- Who is the best listener?

- Who gives the best advice or feedback?

- Who encourages me the most?

- Who inspires me?

- Who helps me feel calm and relaxed?

- Who do I have the most fun with?

Physically Active Coping Skills

- What activities bring me the most joy?

- What activities help my mind relax?

- What sports, hobbies, or interests are most helpful to my mental, emotional, and/or physical health?

- After which activities do I feel most invigorated or clear-headed?

- What activities inspire or motivate me?

Mental/Emotional Processing Coping Skills

- What helps me release or process difficult emotions (e.g., dancing, music, art, journaling, painting, coloring, drawing)?

- What accomplishments or achievements am I most proud of? Bring these to mind when you're overwhelmed, uncertain, or nervous to shift your mood and perspective!

- What do I like about myself?

- What qualities or characteristics have other people complimented me for?

- If I were looking at myself from an outside perspective, what would I say are my strengths?

- What person, character, actor/actress, superhero, entertainer, singer, or role model do I admire most? During times of stress, it can be helpful to "channel" an admirable person (real or theatrical) and ask yourself, *"What would this person do in this situation? How would he/she respond?"* Tuning into another person or character can circumvent your own insecurities, as it's no longer "you" but the character that is responding or dealing with the difficult situation.

Body-Based Coping Skills

- Where do I hold tension, anxiety, sadness, grief, overwhelm, and fear in my body? Some people experience anxiety as a pit in their stomach and grief as a heaviness in their chest. Knowing where you hold these emotions in your body can help you choose coping skills that will address that specific feeling most effectively.

- Do a mental body scan starting from the tips of your toes to the top of your head. Notice any sensations, like heaviness, tingling, aching, or numbness along the way. You can do this any time or whenever you notice that something feels off, but you're not sure exactly where you're feeling it.

- Deep breathing can be used intentionally during a mindful meditation or to reset your nervous system throughout the day. Practice 5-2-5 breathing,[9] which means inhaling for a count of five, holding your breath for a count of two, and exhaling for a count of five. You can repeat this breathing pattern however many times you'd like until you feel calmer, less anxious, or more centered.

- Grounding[10] is a mindfulness-based technique that involves becoming aware of your five senses. This can be especially helpful if you're ruminating about a difficult situation. Take a moment to pause and ask yourself, *"What are five things I can see, four things I can feel, three things I can hear, two things I can smell, and one thing I can taste?"*

- Going on a mindfulness walk can be very calming, especially if you have a sensitive or easily activated nervous system. Find a peaceful place to go outside, ideally in a quiet, serene, and aesthetically pleasing environment, and walk around, intentionally noticing what you can see, hear, touch, taste, and smell. Whenever your mind wanders away from your current environment, gently bring your focus back to the present moment.

Distraction-Based Coping Skills

- What activities or interests can I become mentally and emotionally immersed in?

- How do I usually distract myself from uncomfortable emotions?

- What helps me stop ruminating, even for a short period of time?

- Investing in new, interesting, or slightly challenging hobbies or goals can be very healthy distraction-based coping skills. Learning a new skill or diving into an area of interest can help you regain a sense of mastery, achievement, confidence, or purpose, especially if you're going through a life transition or are dealing with a situation that requires endurance, like co-parenting with a narcissist, switching careers, or ending a relationship.

Environmental/External Supports

- What types of environments overwhelm me?

- What time of day am I the calmest? Why?

- What types of surroundings bring me the most peace?

- How can I incorporate these environmental supports into my daily life? For example, if you feel calmest in nature, you could add lavender-scented candles, nature paintings, or plants to your home.

- What books, shows, podcasts, songs, or movies help me feel happy, calm, inspired, or comforted?

Answer these questions in written form to create your individualized coping skills plan. Keep this list close by, like in your nightstand or office drawer, so you can quickly reference it as needed. Or take a picture of it and save it on your phone for easy access!

I included distraction-based and processing-based coping skills because you really need both. Distraction is not necessarily a bad thing. It can help you stop ruminating about things you can't control or give your nervous system a break from particularly intense emotions like anxiety, panic, or heavy grief.

During these moments, it might be too overwhelming to dive into what you're feeling and why. Instead, you might need to focus on something else for a short time until you become less emotionally charged and can think more clearly.

As you're answering these questions, you might notice that you've been using healthy and unhealthy coping skills. It's important to recognize your current coping skills and replace the ones that have negative side effects. For example, drinking alcohol or scrolling social media are ways people numb their emotions or distract themselves from uncontrollable situations. However, excessive drinking or social media consumption does much more harm than good. Short-term coping skills should not have long-term negative consequences, and if they do, it's time to find healthier alternatives.

This phase is all about creating routines and habits that meet your needs. I encourage you to set daily reminders on your phone to ask yourself, *"How am I feeling right now? What do I need?"* and then journal daily or weekly about the results.

Once you've answered these questions, you have a go-to coping skills list that you can use whenever you need to. It might take days, weeks, or months to complete this list, and that's totally okay! In fact, I recommend reviewing and updating this list once a year, as what you need changes with time.

HOW A STRONG SELF-RELATIONSHIP PROTECTS YOU FROM NARCISSISTS

Healing core wounds, recognizing your emotions, and learning to meet your needs is a process. As I mentioned before, there's no timeline for healing. Let this be the one area of your life that you don't set a deadline for! Honestly, we're always a work in progress. To learn and grow is to live. Let healing become a way of life, not a destination.

Continually investing in your healing isn't just a "good idea"—it's also a narcissist-repellant. Because with narcissists, your blind spots are your vulnerabilities. Narcissists take your subconscious insecurities, worries, or fears, feed them back to you, and say that *those* are the cause of the relationship issues. If you don't know why something is a trigger for you, then you mistakenly assume that the narcissist is right and that the relationship issues *are* your fault.

But if you understand yourself, your triggers, and your insecurities, then you take your power back. You can differentiate between your triggers and your partner's toxic behaviors. You can confidently say, *"I know that's a trigger for me, but what my partner did is still not okay."*

Ultimate healing and self-protection come from understanding narcissistic behaviors (which we did in the first part of this book) *and* knowing and accepting yourself (which is what we will spend the rest of this book accomplishing)!

WRAPPING UP YOUR SELF-RELATIONSHIP

Now that you're moving forward with healing, you need to protect your progress. And you do that best—with *boundaries*. The next chapter will explore what boundaries look like and feel like and how to set and keep them, especially if you're a sensitive, highly empathetic person.

CHAPTER TEN

Boundaries: Your Most Powerful Protection Strategy

"Setting boundaries has been a significant part of my healing. I have set boundaries for the privacy of my home, hand-off/drop-off with the kids, how I respond to text information and content, and the 'time-urgency' to respond to emails from my ex-narc. I am better able to think and reflect and respond in an objective, factual way without involving emotions and feelings. It is very much like a 'business transaction,' and it leads to less confrontation, offering less of me to control and manipulate. I keep it brief, factual, informative, and objective. I have also set boundaries with my time (who I want to spend time with and who has access to my life and information)."
–Anonymous

Boundaries: you know you need them, but what are they, *really*? And how do you create healthy ones if you don't have them? There are many types of boundaries: physical, mental/emotional, sexual, financial, and time/energy boundaries. For our purposes, we'll focus on setting mental/emotional boundaries, as these are relentlessly pushed in toxic relationships. Plus, once you feel confident setting mental and emotional boundaries, you can expand that understanding and practice to all the other boundary types.

To start, you need to understand what a boundary feels like. The easiest way to do this is to think about when someone is in your personal space. When someone crosses a physical boundary, you're immediately aware of it. It's as if your body is screaming, *"Too close! Back up!"* You feel vulnerable, invaded, uncomfortable, and sometimes even annoyed, angry, or scared. We describe this as someone being "in your bubble."

I like to think of not just physical boundaries but all boundaries as a "bubble" that surrounds you. Here's what I mean: when you're with healthy people, you feel free to move around in your bubble and for them to move around in theirs. You don't feel guilty for having your thoughts, feelings, and opinions, you respect each other's space, time, and energy, and you recognize that you can't control anything that's outside your bubble.

However, when you're with toxic people, you feel as if your bubble is being squeezed from the outside. You feel pressured to agree with the other person and guilty if you don't. You feel judged, criticized, or shamed for how you move around in your bubble. And you find yourself expanding your bubble, trying to manage, take responsibility for, or fix other people and their problems, which leaves you feeling stretched too thin and like you're about to burst.

Your bubble *is* your boundary. Anytime you feel pressured, your bubble (i.e., boundary) is being pushed. And anytime you feel like you're about to burst, your boundary is expanding beyond what's healthy. With healthy boundaries, you feel:

- Calm
- Secure

- Self-assured

- Safe

- Stable

With unhealthy boundaries, you feel:

- Exhausted

- Overwhelmed

- Confused

- Lonely

- Misunderstood

- Used

- Pressured

- Anxious/Frantic

Healthy boundaries are flexible, balanced, and well-grounded. You feel safe to share your opinion, respect others' choices, meet others' needs, and communicate your own. Think of healthy boundaries like pool lane dividers: they're firm enough to stay intact but flexible enough to allow the water (i.e., yours and others' emotions/needs) to flow back and forth.

Rigid boundaries are inflexible, isolating, and overly self-protective. When your boundaries are too rigid, you keep people at a distance, don't share even when it's safe to, avoid getting too close, and rarely, if ever, ask for help. You isolate and avoid people because you don't know how to feel safe when you're around others. Think of rigid boundaries like a closed door with no handle: nothing is getting in or out.

Enmeshed boundaries (also referred to as porous or diffuse boundaries) leave you feeling exposed, unprotected, and internally chaotic. When you have enmeshed boundaries, you feel personally responsible for others' issues, tolerate or make excuses for abusive behaviors, try to "save" others, blame yourself for things outside of your control, and rarely, if ever, say "No."

When you're around people, you do whatever will create the least number of waves. Porous boundaries are like a swimming pool with no dividers. Everyone's emotions, perspectives, expectations, and wants all get thrown into the same water with nothing to separate *others'* needs from *your* needs.

HOW DID YOU DEVELOP YOUR CURRENT BOUNDARIES?

Much like an inner critic, you weren't *born* with bad boundaries. And that's a good thing! Because this means that no matter what boundaries you have now, *you can change them.*

During childhood, boundaries are like invisible rules you learn to follow. Most of the time, you're not taught about them explicitly. Instead, boundaries are woven into your understanding of reality so that you don't even recognize or question them until you're harmed by having unhealthy boundaries. Based on hundreds of survivors' stories and thousands of hours working with clients, I've noticed four major influences on boundary development:

- What you observe from caregivers/parents
- Your role in the family system
- Your individual personality style
- Cultural/traditional/religious principles

OBSERVATIONS: WHAT WAS "NORMAL" IN YOUR FAMILY?

As a child, you would describe a boundary as "how things are." Boundaries tell you what can or can't be said at the dinner table. They say which topics can be discussed and which topics are off-limits. They tell you how to respond to the emotions of others and your own. Boundaries that are crossed or ignored lead to consequences or punishments. Boundaries that are followed result in praise, attention, and loyalty.

Learning to identify your current boundaries means learning to recognize the types of boundaries that were common in your family of origin. To get started, reflect on or journal about these questions regarding your childhood home:

- Growing up, what was the emotional temperature (e.g., cold and rigid, warm and friendly, etc.) of your home?
- Were family members allowed to agree to disagree?
- Was stonewalling or the silent treatment ever used as a form of punishment/consequence?
- Were discussions about emotions a normal part of life?
- Did your caregivers ever use guilt to control you?

- Was love conditional or unconditional in your family? How can you tell?

- What were the "house rules?"

- What were the expectations around discussing family issues with those outside the home? Was it allowed, encouraged, reprimanded, or completely off-limits?

- Who had the final say in your household? How did this person enforce family rules or expectations? What happened if someone violated (intentionally or unintentionally) those rules?

- Was there ever inappropriate physical/sexual touch between family members?

- Were family members respectful of each other's time, possessions, physical space, and/or personal beliefs?

- If there was more than one child, was everyone reasonably treated the same, or were there obvious differences between how each child was treated?

- Did one or more family members enable another member to behave in toxic, dysfunctional, abusive, or addictive ways?

Your answers to a lot of these questions might be "sometimes" or "it depends." And if so, that's okay! Be as detailed as you can when answering these questions, explaining any exceptions or nuances. The goal is to bring conscious awareness to your family's patterns so you can see the impact these interactions had on your boundary development.

Keep in mind that it's possible your family members displayed unpredictable or mixed boundaries, meaning they were sometimes rigid, sometimes enmeshed, and sometimes healthy.

Mixed boundaries can be especially confusing since you don't know what to expect. If you can relate to never being sure of the mood your parent would be in, your family likely had mixed boundaries. This is not uncommon in households with substance use issues, intense/untreated mental health issues, addictions, or personality disorders.[1]

HOW FAMILY PATTERNS AFFECT YOUR BOUNDARIES

Certain family patterns lead to the development of different boundaries. For example, if you were given the silent treatment for disagreeing with someone, then you learned that to be loved and cared for, you had to agree. This could lead to enmeshed boundaries in adulthood since you're afraid that disagreeing with someone means they won't love you anymore.

On the other hand, if there was a lot of chaos, manipulation, or neglect, you could develop rigid boundaries to protect yourself from being taken advantage of or neglected.

Family patterns that often lead to the development of enmeshed boundaries in adulthood include:

- Cultural beliefs like "Family comes first" or "What happens in the family stays in the family."
- Allowing or enabling neglectful or abusive behaviors.

- Being shamed or guilted if you disagree or go against family customs, traditions, or beliefs.

- Consistent patterns of oversharing between family members.

- Religious beliefs that enforce the idea that setting boundaries makes you "selfish" or "bad."

- Chaotic, unstable, or dysfunctional environments where you never know what to expect.

- Frequent statements like, "I only worry because I care so much," or "I can only be happy if you're happy."

- Use of guilt trips to control behaviors (e.g., "If you loved me, you would...").

Family patterns that often lead to the development of rigid boundaries in adulthood include:

- Frequent relocation to new places, schools, or houses.

- Extremely high values or unreasonable expectations placed on being self-sufficient or independent.

- Active drug, sex, or alcohol addictions in family members.

- Minimal physical affection or nurturance.

- Detached, permissive, uninvolved, or neglectful parenting styles.

- Frequent use of harsh or developmentally inappropriate criticisms.

- Use of mixed or unpredictable boundaries.

- Instances of inappropriate physical and/or sexual touch.

Family patterns that often lead to the development of healthy boundaries in adulthood include:

- Consistent routines and schedules.
- Authoritative parenting styles.
- Frequent displays of nurturing and encouraging interactions.
- Knowing what to expect from family members (i.e., calm reactions, reliable behaviors, stable emotions, etc.).
- Modeling of healthy emotional regulation and use of appropriate coping skills.
- Allowance for different viewpoints and emphasis on respectful communication.
- Encouragement of self-reflection and exploration of individual values, beliefs, and opinions.
- Respect for others' personal space, possessions, thoughts, feelings, and beliefs.

Reflect on these family patterns and see which ones resonate with you. This will help you determine what "reality" looked like in your family, what you learned to expect in relationships, and the beliefs you formed about what you "should" or "shouldn't" say, think, or feel.

FAMILY ROLES: WHAT WAS EXPECTED OF YOU?

Think of the role you played in your family. Were you the peacemaker, caretaker, entertainer, or free spirit? Were you overly scolded and consistently labeled the "problem?" Did you feel invisible or irrelevant? How were you expected to behave, feel, or think? Give yourself some time to journal about the following questions to uncover these unspoken expectations.

- How did your parents/caregivers respond when you expressed a need or an emotion?

- Were some emotions allowed while others were discouraged? For example, maybe you were allowed to be sad but discouraged from being angry.

- Did you ever feel like you were responsible for other family members' emotions or reactions? How so?

- Did your parents talk to you about adult situations or issues?

- Did you feel comfortable having or expressing an opinion that was different from the adults in your home?

- Did you feel safe and comfortable asking for help from your family? Why or why not?

- How were you treated differently than your siblings or other family members? Were you expected to feel, think, or behave in certain ways?

- What was your role in the family (e.g., peacemaker, scapegoat, helper, invisible child, golden child, truth teller, troublemaker, nurturer, rescuer, mediator, comedian, etc.)?

- What makes you believe/feel this was your role?

- What's your birth order (i.e., oldest, middle, youngest, only child)? What was it like being the (oldest, middle, youngest, or only) in your family?

These reflections help you answer the question, "What was it like to be **me** in my family?" This is highly important because your current boundaries are largely based on what you believe you need to do to be safe, loved, and accepted.

For example, if you were allowed to be an independent thinker and feel your feelings, then you likely feel *safe* setting healthy boundaries. If, however, you were shown love for being a people-pleaser, then you were *rewarded* for having unhealthy boundaries. This creates a belief that to feel loved, you must *ignore* your boundaries and needs.

When you're in an unhealthy family system, you're shamed for doing what's healthy. Toxic people don't want you to have healthy boundaries because it makes you harder to manipulate.

This is why recognizing how you felt growing up is so essential to set healthy boundaries in the present. Because if unhealthy boundaries were the norm in your family of origin, then initially, setting healthy boundaries by saying "No," agreeing to disagree, or holding fast to your beliefs will feel wrong, bad, or even sinful at first.

Another theme you might notice when answering these questions is that you felt responsible for things outside of your control. Maybe you were expected to care for younger siblings even though you were still a child. Maybe your parent(s) talked to you about adult matters or discussed their marital issues with you. The process of children taking on adult responsibilities is called *parentification*.

Parentification is more likely to occur with emotionally immature parents and/or sensitive or empathetic children.[2] Parentification has a big impact on boundary development as the child learns that the emotional intimacy of the relationship *increases* with more responsibilities. Essentially, the more the child does for the parent, the more the parent pays attention to, appreciates, or acknowledges the child.

This is a direct setup for enmeshed boundaries in adulthood. You become so accustomed to "doing it all" that unbalanced relationships feel normal. Naturally, this is an opening for narcissistic individuals who are always seeking an unhealthy amount of support and help.

PERSONALITY STYLE: HOW COMFORTABLE ARE YOU WITH CONFLICT?

Some people seem to be born more comfortable with conflict. And, in fact, that's true! Temperament[3] is the biological component of personality and accounts for things like emotional reactivity, sensitivity to environmental stimuli, and level of agreeableness.

Some people are born with a predisposition to be more disagreeable, while others are born more agreeable and sensitive to their surroundings. Those with sensitive temperaments are more likely to be empaths, introverts, and/or highly sensitive persons.[4]

Reflect on these questions to learn how much your temperament has impacted your aversion to setting healthy boundaries:

- On a scale of 1–10, how intensely are you bothered by conflict?

- What have you been willing to sacrifice (e.g., your happiness, time, money) to avoid possible conflict?

- How long does it take you to calm down after a disagreement?

- Can you relax if someone is upset with you, even if you haven't done anything wrong?

If you easily feel others' emotions, are drained by busy environments, avoid the possibility of conflict even to your own detriment, and frequently become anxious or overwhelmed, you likely have a sensitive temperament.[5]

Many times (especially in toxic relationships), you silently ponder the question, *"Is saying/doing this worth the conflict I know it will create?"*

Setting boundaries with a sensitive temperament can be challenging since your initial reaction is to "keep the peace." And from a biological standpoint, you're motivated to do so! For those with sensitive nervous systems, dealing with others' disappointments is personally distressing. But you *can* become more comfortable setting healthy boundaries, even with a sensitive temperament. Keep reading to see how!

(Aside from your temperament, trauma can also be a reason you feel hesitant or paralyzed to set healthy boundaries. If the idea of setting boundaries makes you feel nauseous, panicky, or numb, please know you can take this process at a pace that feels manageable for you. Healing from trauma will help you in setting boundaries, too.)

MORAL/RELIGIOUS PRINCIPLES: WHAT DOES IT MEAN TO BE A "GOOD PERSON?"

Traditional roles. Moral principles. Cultural expectations. Religious beliefs. None of these are bad within themselves; in fact, they can be very good. But too often, these values, beliefs, and expectations are twisted to shame and control people's behaviors, especially from parent to child.

For example, sometimes religious doctrine is used to shame children into obedience, or cultural expectations are used as justifications for dysfunctional or abusive behaviors.

As a child, it's natural to assume that these stringent guidelines must be followed to be a good, moral, or productive person. Unfortunately, the effect is often a perpetual feeling of uncertainty, shame, rejection, worthlessness, and inadequacy.

Did you hear any of these statements growing up?

- "Real men don't cry."
- "Kids should be seen and not heard."
- "How you feel isn't important."
- "What happens in the family stays in the family."
- "Good children respect their parents no matter what."
- "Everyone deserves a second chance."
- "You should always put others' needs ahead of your own."
- "A good wife follows her husband in everything."
- "That's just how things are done in our culture."
- "A good husband keeps his family together."

- "Love means you never give up."

- "A good person gives without expecting anything in return."

- "Only selfish people think about their own needs."

Family systems with unhealthy boundaries often have negative views of families who set healthy ones. For example, families who have enmeshed boundaries label those who set healthy boundaries as uncaring, harsh, or rude. Families who have rigid boundaries describe healthy families as coddling, enabling, or spoiling their children.

Many cultural, religious, or traditional expectations are passed down with the best of intentions. But the piece that's usually missing … is healthy boundaries.

Giving is great—but what do you do when you meet a perpetual taker? Forgiveness is a gift—but what do you do when someone views your forgiveness as permission to keep hurting you?

When you're raised to believe that being a good person means giving, forgiving, and assuming the best, you're left at a complete loss as to what to do with the difficult, cruel, and toxic people of the world.

So, you try to make sense of toxic behaviors through the only framework you have: "People make mistakes," "Everyone deserves a second chance," or "You can't expect someone to be perfect."

And these are usually the same justifications you use to tolerate abusive behaviors or stay with a narcissist despite the cost.

HOW TO SET HEALTHY BOUNDARIES (EVEN IF YOU'RE HIGHLY SENSITIVE)

"Just realizing that I could set limits on people without having to explain myself makes me feel that I have an internal parent who cares about me. And surprisingly, most people respond quite positively to boundaries. I gained control over my life, and continue to feel more in harmony as I practice boundary setting."
–Anonymous

Boundary setting is like a muscle—the more you use it, the stronger (and easier) it gets. If you haven't consistently practiced *intentional* boundary setting, then the thought of this process likely feels uncomfortable, overwhelming, intimidating, or even terrifying. And that's okay! We all start somewhere.

I imagine you're reading this book because you've either desperately needed boundaries in the past or desperately need them currently, which means you're already familiar with being uncomfortable. The discomfort of boundary setting is time-limited, purposeful, and intentional. You can choose to remain *permanently* uncomfortable by not having healthy boundaries or *temporarily* uncomfortable by learning to set them.

Much like how building a self-relationship starts with self-reflection, setting boundaries starts with awareness-building, too. Start being curious about your current boundaries. Before you act, respond, or make a decision, ask yourself:

- "Why am I doing this?"
- "Do I have the emotional capacity for this?"
- "Will other areas of my life suffer if I do this?"

- "Can I directly control this?"

- "If I can't directly control this, what can I really do here?"

- "Is this my issue to fix, or is someone else wanting me to do what only they can do?"

- "Does this decision feel safe, healthy, and good for me?"

- "Can I do this in a way that would feel safe, healthy, and good for me?" (For example, agreeing to help, but only for a certain amount of time.)

- "Does this relationship feel balanced?"

- "If I do this, how will I feel about myself?"

These questions illuminate your current boundaries and guide you to see the areas in your life that are balanced and unbalanced. You might find that you have healthy boundaries with one person and enmeshed boundaries with another. Give yourself time and space to explore these questions from a nonjudgmental stance.

DISPELLING THE MYTH: "I DON'T HAVE ANY BOUNDARIES."

Many people feel overwhelmed with the idea of boundary setting because they feel like they don't have *any* at this point. But everyone has boundaries, even if they're not where you want them to be. Locking your doors at night, having a passcode on your phone, and not giving your neighbor access to your bank account are all boundaries. It's important to recognize the places you *already* have boundaries, give yourself credit for those choices, and grow from there.

BOUNDARY TIP: DON'T SELF-SABOTAGE

One of the biggest mistakes people make when setting boundaries is starting with their most intimate relationships *first*. However, boundary lines are often blurriest in close relationships. Starting there is like trying to run a marathon when you haven't even finished a 5k. If the outcome you want seems overwhelming, impossible, or hopeless, you're likely to give up too soon. But you *will* get there; you just shouldn't *start* there.

BOUNDARY SETTING: PRACTICAL STRATEGIES

Step 1: Set Silent Boundaries

Silent boundaries are boundaries that no one even knows you're setting ... except you. If vocalizing your emotions, needs, or expectations feels too big right now, practice mentally rehearsing them in your mind. Think to yourself, *"I don't agree with that," "I don't think that,"* or *"That's not how I feel."* Identify in your mind what you *do* think or how you *do* feel.

The first step in boundary setting is identifying, allowing, and exploring *your* thoughts, feelings, and beliefs. Acknowledge, even silently, that your experiences and emotions are just as valid as anyone else's.

Step 2: Start Small

When you're learning a new concept or implementing a new strategy (especially ones that are emotionally charged), it's easy to go from one extreme to the next. For example, if you've felt the pain of enmeshed boundaries, you might decide that "No one will ever take advantage of me again," or "I'll never let myself be vulnerable."

However, this can push you too far the other way, where you end up setting very rigid boundaries.

To counteract this urge to swing from one extreme to the other, you need to *start small*. Set boundaries in areas that feel less risky or where the outcomes don't feel so significant. You can also be more intentional or firmer with the boundaries you already have. You can do things like:

- Engage in the hobbies you enjoy at least one time a week.

- Bring a friend when you go to new places.

- Spend five minutes meditating in the car after work before driving home.

- Share your opinion when discussing trivial topics (e.g., movies, music, favorite flower, etc.).

- Be more observant instead of jumping to fix someone's problem.

- Ask how you can help instead of assuming what someone needs.

- Smile and say, "No, thank you!"

- Tell your waiter if you received the wrong/incorrect order.

- State your opinion even if you know/think the other person will disagree.

- Just say less—if normally you would go over the top with explaining, congratulating, or fixing, do less of that.

- Stop being so available.

These examples might feel easy for some and difficult for others, but I wanted to show you how boundaries can be set anywhere and everywhere. Boundaries don't have to mean making big, bold, and scary changes. Any decision you make that feels safe and healthy *is* a boundary.

It's also important to note that boundaries and self-care work in tandem with each other. One of the biggest obstacles to consistent self-care is poor boundaries, and vice versa, so the better you get at one, the more the other will improve as well.

Step 3: Be Prepared

Nothing stops boundary setting quicker than feeling overwhelmed or hopeless. That's why having boundary-conscious statements in mind is essential, particularly in the beginning stages. This also helps combat a very real threat to boundary setting called *decision fatigue*,[6] which means the more decisions you make, the more depleted you feel. And the more depleted you feel, the more likely you are to fall back into old, familiar patterns.

If setting healthy boundaries is new to you, it's going to take more conscious effort *at first,* which means you need to make setting healthy boundaries as easy as possible. The easier it is to set a boundary, the more likely you are to follow through.

Consider memorizing a few of the following statements/responses to make setting boundaries less taxing on your mental and emotional energy reserves.

- "I'll have to check my schedule."
- "Let me get back to you on that."

- "I'm sorry, I have a previous commitment."

- "I'd love to, but I can't this time. Can we find a different day to connect?"

- "I appreciate the invite, but I already have plans that day!"

- "That's a really generous offer, but I'd like to take care of this myself."

- "That's an interesting request. Let me think on it and get back to you."

- "That question will require some thought. I'll be in touch!"

- "Unfortunately, I won't be able to make it at that time, but I can put it in my calendar for next week."

- "My schedule books out a couple weeks in advance, but if you'd like to give me a time that works for you in the future, I can save that spot for you."

- "I want to give you a thoughtful response. Can you check back with me on that next week?"

These responses follow a basic formula: appreciate or acknowledge the request, set your boundary, then offer another solution, praise their efforts, or change the subject.

Generally, you don't have to respond to someone's request or statement right away. If you know the answer you'd like to give but need time to think about how to say it tactfully, let them know you'll get back to them the next day or next week. If you feel completely caught off guard by someone's request, respond with something like "That's interesting," "I haven't thought about it like that before," or "I'll need to think about that one."

Remember, you're not obligated to give someone something just because they ask (or because you can intuit what they want). You're not here for the sole purpose of meeting everyone else's needs. You're a human being—with your own thoughts, feelings, and opinions that should be considered. Make sure you give yourself the same amount of grace, understanding, and patience you give everyone else.

WHAT TO EXPECT WHEN YOU SET HEALTHY BOUNDARIES

Healthy boundaries *will* improve your life. But not everyone will act like it. Remember, healthy boundaries don't keep the healthy people out—just the toxic ones. This means toxic people will push back on your boundaries *the most*.

While practicing intentional boundary setting, observe who respects these changes and who doesn't. Don't let the fact that you experience conflict or tension make you think you're doing something wrong. More than likely, the people who dislike your boundaries are the same ones who benefit from your *lack* of boundaries.

HOW BOUNDARIES CHANGE YOUR LIFE

Boundaries do so much more than improve your self-esteem and reveal the toxic people in your life. Healthy boundaries have an impact on your happiness and overall life satisfaction.[7] They protect you from burnout, fatigue, and stress.[8] They help you ruminate less, sleep better, and regulate your emotions more effectively.[9]

But more than anything, boundaries prove that *you matter*. When you think to yourself, *"I don't agree,"* you give yourself permission to feel your feelings. When you say "No," you show yourself that you're allowed to be different. When you give your opinion (even if it's different from others), you teach yourself that your value isn't based on agreeing with someone.

The very act of setting a boundary is evidence that *you're worth protecting*. And for some, that's a new concept.

If you didn't feel protected, cared for, validated, or understood growing up, this is the time to show your inner child that he/she *is* good enough. And every time you set a boundary, you do just that.

WRAPPING UP BOUNDARIES

You made it through parts one and two! How are you feeling? Take a moment to reflect on or journal about what you've learned so far. When you're ready, part three is next. We'll cover the biggest supports and blocks to healing, as well as how to catapult your post-traumatic growth.

PART THREE

HEALING YOUR PAST, PRESENT, AND FUTURE

CHAPTER ELEVEN

Healing: Mindset Shifts You Need to Make

"Value who you are as a person and know that nobody on this earth has the right to belittle you and make you feel worthless."
–Claire

Are you a different person today than you were six months ago? A year ago? Ten years ago? My guess is your answer is an emphatic "Yes." We see a lot of changes in ourselves when we look back, yet we tend to underestimate how different we will be in the future. This tendency is called the end of history illusion[1] and being aware of this concept is vital to your healing.

In this moment, you might find it very difficult to imagine yourself ever feeling differently than you do right now. And that's okay. Abuse and trauma have a way of shrinking our vision and magnifying our present challenges.

But can you widen your vision enough to see the *possibility* of healing? Because research and time show us that in the future, who we are and how we feel will change—and much more significantly than we predict it will.

You aren't the same person today that you were five years ago, and in five years, you won't be the same person that you are today. Who you are now is based on what you've been through up to this point, but who you *will be* is based on what you do *today*.

Even if, right now, you feel like it's impossible to leave your narcissistic relationship, set boundaries, or experience more peace, you won't necessarily feel that way in six months because you'll be a *different* **you**.

Think of it like this: if you didn't believe the ocean existed, you wouldn't bother taking the trip; but you *know* the ocean is real, so you trust your GPS to get you there.

In this scenario, a *healed you* is the ocean, and this book is the GPS. Trust the process and take the steps toward growth, even though you haven't seen the ocean yet. This moment is about shifting your mindset from feeling like you *must* have everything figured out to being willing to *take a step*.

You don't need the sun to illuminate your whole path; you just need a flashlight to illuminate it one step at a time. Let this book be your flashlight and take your healing one day at a time.

A MINDSET FOR HEALING

Healing is a process—not a checklist. The idea that there is a right or wrong way to heal is a continuance of the perfectionist mindset—a mindset that no doubt is intensified by being with a narcissist. Healing is about keeping your eyes on the ground and putting one foot in front of the other. You don't need to look up and compare yourself to everyone else. You don't need to look around every day to see if you're making enough progress.

You need to focus on taking care of yourself, understanding what you've been through, and trusting the process. You might not be where you want to be, but you're also not where you were. Give yourself some breathing room, and with time, support, and self-compassion, your future self will be further along than your current self ever thought possible.

During this healing journey, you'll have moments of hope and moments of despair. Some days you'll wonder if you're growing at all, and other days, you'll realize how much progress you've made. To prepare for the inevitable hills and valleys, you need to be equipped with the right mindset.

If you know ahead of time the journey will be rough, then you're not caught off guard when you hit bumpy roads. It's my hope that the following sections will normalize the emotions, struggles, and doubts that are sure to happen during your healing journey.

Mindset Shift #1: Healing is possible whether you stay or go.

If leaving the narcissist (or going no contact) isn't a viable option in your situation, you might wonder: *is healing even possible for me?* One big misconception is that you can't get better if you *stay* with the narcissist or if the narcissist is someone you deal with regularly, like through co-parenting, family events, or work relationships.

But this is not true.

You can still find moments of happiness and contentment. You can still learn to talk kindly to yourself, meet your emotional needs, and appreciate your strengths. You can still form healthy relationships, have fun, enjoy a movie, or engage in meaningful hobbies.

I say this with a heavy heart, knowing that healing *is* more challenging if you stay or must have some form of regular contact with the narcissist.

However, *this doesn't mean you have no hope of a happy and fulfilling life*. Healing can take many forms and looks different for different people.

For some, healing means not letting the narcissist completely ruin your day. For others, healing means disengaging once the narcissist becomes contemptuous or leaving the room when you're feeling judged.

As Victor Frankl said in his groundbreaking book, *Man's Search for Meaning*, "Everything can be taken from a man but one thing: the last of the human freedoms—to choose one's attitude in any given set of circumstances, to choose one's own way." And to think that this mindset came from a man who suffered the Nazi concentration camps and saw horrors most of us can only imagine!

Frankl noticed that prisoners who focused on what they *could* control (e.g., relationships with other survivors) and found *purpose* in the camp (e.g., being an encourager) fared much better mentally, emotionally, and oftentimes physically than those who spent most of their time focused on the environment.

We can't underestimate the healing power of finding meaning, even through, during, and after suffering. Don't give away your power to heal to the abuser—they don't deserve it. It's *your turn* to determine your fate.

Mindset Shift #2: Anger is not a bad emotion. It's an essential part of healing.

Sometimes we hold ourselves hostage from healing because we think anger shouldn't be the motivator for change. You might think, *"I don't want to stay angry,"* or *"I shouldn't feel this angry."* Or you might even struggle to *feel* angry at all.

But anger is a normal and healthy reaction to abuse and injustice. If you have a hard time feeling angry about the abuse you've experienced (or hesitate to even call it "abuse"), you probably also have a hard time feeling worthy or good enough.

If you've ever felt angry about witnessing an injustice done to someone else but struggle to feel angry about the things you've been through, then you understand exactly what I mean.

Feeling angry means something happened that shouldn't have happened. But if part of you feels like you deserved mistreatment or somehow are responsible for the abuse because you "should've known better," then you'll shut down anger as soon as it arises.

It's as if your subconscious is saying, *"I don't have a right to feel angry. I should've been able to handle this. Was it even really abuse? I mean, how could I have been abused if I was part of the problem?"*

It's important to allow yourself to feel angry about abuses or traumas you've been through or are experiencing. In fact, as you heal and set healthier boundaries, you'll likely notice that you feel angrier more often. This can be a sign that you're starting to feel more self-worth as you start to believe that you *didn't* deserve to be abused, manipulated, lied to, or rejected.

Anger can be a great motivator for change. Anger can give you the strength to leave an abusive situation. It can motivate you to do everything the narcissist said you couldn't do. It can embolden you with a spirit of "I'll show you."

And sometimes, that's exactly where healing starts. Every fire needs a spark to burst into flames. This doesn't mean you'll stay angry, but don't be afraid to allow anger to push you toward positive change.

If, on the other hand, you've been angry for a very long time and don't feel it's getting any better, it might be time to seek therapy, coaching, or some form of professional help.

Chronic anger can lead to physical problems and other mental and emotional health issues.[2] Plus, long-term anger means your mental and emotional energy is still largely going to the narcissist.

But healing is about collecting that energy and redirecting it toward *you* and your life, goals, and needs, and investing it in healthy relationships.

Mindset Shift #3: You are **not** who the narcissist said you were.

Narcissists *tell you* who you are. They pigeonhole your emotions, reactions, behaviors, and traits in a way that benefits them and makes you easier to manipulate. They relabel your empathy as weakness, your consistency as boring, and your conscientiousness as controlling.

If they can make you believe you're someone you're not, then you will rely on *them* to guide you. They condition you to believe that they are the truth—but they are the biggest lie of all.

Healing means *knowing* you are **not** who they said you were. Make a list of everything the narcissist criticized you for (e.g., being too sensitive, weak, needy, controlling, stupid, jealous) and find a way to purposefully *prove them wrong*.

Start by giving yourself credit for the things you already do. For example, showing kindness to your pets, calling to check on your parents, volunteering for your child's class field trip, getting up on days when you don't feel like it, or getting to work on time show that you are compassionate, caring, resilient, and respectful.

This process is about **you** *defining* **you**. For too long, the narcissist has tried to undermine, criticize, and control not only your behaviors, feelings, and self-talk but also your goals and aspirations.

Narcissists scoff at and degrade your abilities, telling you that you aren't capable or smart enough to go to college, finish your degree program, secure a job, ask for a promotion, start a business, write a book, or any personally meaningful goal.

Write down the goals you didn't finish or pursue due to the narcissist's demeaning comments or willful interference. Then, take small, intentional steps toward achieving those goals or create new ones based on your current interests. You might start researching degree programs, enroll in a course, read a book on starting a business, begin searching for your preferred job, or write an outline for your book.

When affirmations are based on ideals (e.g., "I'm the healthiest I've ever been," or "I have my dream job"), you feel like you're lying to yourself. But when affirmations are based on action, *you can believe them*. This is vital to healing because it's not in your head; it's what you're *doing*. Your brain can see proof of who you are. And as you begin to *act* differently, you'll *see* yourself differently, which means you'll *feel* differently, too. And *that* is what healing is all about.

In the end, whether you complete these goals as you originally intended isn't as important as taking the steps to start. The real end goal is to show yourself that the narcissist no longer gets a voice in your life. And that what you do or don't do will be because of *your* choices and not because of anything the narcissist said.

Mindset Shift #4: Having triggers isn't a sign of weakness.

Survivors of narcissistic abuse often feel bad for having triggers. They feel like it proves there's something "wrong" with them or that they're "broken." But triggers don't prove *you* are bad—it proves something you *went through* was bad. Triggers validate your reality. You wouldn't have triggers if you didn't go through something traumatic.

You wouldn't ruminate if it wasn't confusing. You wouldn't walk on eggshells if you weren't criticized. You have flashbacks, bad dreams, and sick-to-your-stomach feelings because what happened wasn't okay.

Feeling uneasy or hypervigilant means you've felt unsafe. Feeling unmotivated or apathetic means you're dealing with something heavy. Feeling numb or paralyzed means you're experiencing something harmful.

Of course, you don't want to feel intense triggers all the time … and healing helps lessen their impact. But triggers aren't the enemy. They don't mean you're broken. They mean what happened was real.

WRAPPING UP MINDSET SHIFTS

Now that you know the necessary mindset shifts to make, let's look at the most common reasons people stay stuck. That way, you have a clear view of what *to* do and *not* to do for your healing.

CHAPTER TWELVE

Blocks to Healing: The Most Common Reasons You Stay Stuck

"Believe in yourself. It's not your fault that things happened the way they did. And don't think you're the crazy one."
–Matthew

Healing isn't just about knowing what to do; it's also about knowing what *not* to do. Here are some of the most common blocks to healing, with guidance on how to move past them.

Healing Block #1: Focusing too much on the pain and not enough on healing.

Narcissistic abuse *hurts*. There's no way around it. Experiencing constant devaluation, criticism, and rejection cuts you to the core. There is a time to see what you've been through and to feel the weight of its gravity on your life. To realize how much it impacted you and to meet that pain with compassion.

But there's a difference between wading through the pain and drowning in it. Healing is about letting your pain *breathe*. Air it out. Give it a voice and let it be seen for what it is.

Pain isn't meant to stay inside of you; it's meant to be seen, held, understood, and redirected toward something meaningful.

As Ehime Ora said, "Resurrect the deep pain within you and give it a place to live that's not within your body. Let it live in art … writing … music. Let it be devoured by building brighter connections. Your body is not a coffin for pain to be buried in. Put it somewhere else."

Give yourself permission to feel the hurt. But also give yourself permission to feel joy, peace, and happiness. Make time to laugh, smile, and be still.

In her bestselling book, *13 Things Mentally Strong People Don't Do*, Amy Morin shares how to create and sustain mental strength and resiliency by discussing what mentally strong people *don't* do. She notes how resilient people "don't focus on things they can't control," "don't worry about pleasing everyone," "don't give up after the first failure," and "don't expect immediate results."

Over time, your attention should shift from the pain the narcissist caused you to the way you overcame it. See yourself as the survivor you are. You're here, reading this book, taking your life back. No one made you decide to heal. You did that *yourself* because you wanted something different for your life. Take ownership of the steps *you* have taken to move forward.

On another note, if you've tried to heal on your own but continue to experience post-traumatic symptoms like flashbacks, intrusive thoughts, difficulty sleeping, or impairment in your daily life, please seek out a licensed psychotherapist to help. These symptoms are nothing to be ashamed of, and we all need help at one point or another. Healing is also about being willing to ask for and accept support, so please, don't hesitate to seek help as you need it.

Healing Block #2: Believing if you miss them, you shouldn't have left.

Have you ever been driving and almost had a wreck? Maybe someone pulled out in front of you, almost rear-ended you, or an animal jumped out onto the road. It's likely that you gasped, held your breath, and instantaneously experienced a surge of adrenaline and an increased heart rate.

And even though you *didn't* end up in a wreck, it still takes a few minutes for your heart rate to return to normal. Obviously, you don't criticize your heart rate for taking a few minutes to return to baseline. You don't get mad at yourself and think, *"I didn't even get in a wreck; I shouldn't still be feeling on edge!"* In fact, to think that seems ridiculous and silly.

And yet, you do just that when you expect yourself not to miss someone you once loved. Judging yourself for taking too long to heal is like judging your heart rate for not immediately returning to baseline after a scary scenario.

Just because you're feeling sad, lonely, anxious, or hopeless *does not mean you're not healing*. These emotions are part of the grief process.

And when you've been in a narcissistic relationship, you have a lot to grieve: the loss of your sense of self, the time you invested in the relationship, the way they treated you, the impact their behaviors have had on you, and much more.

Experience the sadness, anger, and anxiety, and let it be. There's nothing strange or wrong with having mixed emotions. We get in trouble when we make our emotions *mean* something, like that we made a mistake, aren't making any progress, should still be with that person, or missed out on our soulmate.

Initially, your emotions and visceral reactions will not match your logic. Your nervous system craves familiarity, so for a time, it will say, *"I miss them. I made a mistake!"* but your logical mind knows, *"That wasn't healthy—I can't go back."*

You have to decide ahead of time to engage in regular self-care and set healthy boundaries even if some days (or many days) you don't *feel* like doing so.

Don't criticize yourself for having ups and downs when that's exactly what healing feels like.

Healing Block #3: Having rigid, black-and-white thinking patterns.

Believing that there's a right and wrong way to heal is very detrimental to your growth. This frequently happens if you have a perfectionist mindset or are a prepared-for-anything type of person.

Healing is about learning to give yourself grace, compassion, and understanding. It's about realizing that comparisons serve no purpose here. It's about giving yourself credit for what you *are* doing, even if you're not doing everything you'd like to be doing yet.

We often have an idea in our mind of what healing looks like, the emotions we should or shouldn't be having, and a timeline for how long all of this should take. And if we don't meet this subconscious ideal, then we begin to feel panicky, depressed, hopeless, or numb.

Take some time to reflect on what this unspoken ideal is in your mind. That way, you can recognize when you're holding yourself to this standard and intentionally choose to notice what you *have* done.

In truth, there is no external healing standard by which you should be judging yourself. Naturally, there are observable patterns that reflect healthy or unhealthy choices. But believing that you're either succeeding or failing is a continuation of the mindset that developed from being narcissistically abused.

Narcissists treat you in rigid ways. They're either love bombing you or devaluing you, criticizing you or praising you, hoovering you or rejecting you.

Within this environment, you get used to judging yourself on this all-or-nothing scale. This bleeds over into blocking your healing by creating thoughts like:

- *"I shouldn't still feel this way."*
- *"I'm never going to move past this."*
- *"I should be better by now."*
- *"I can never let this happen again."*
- *"I'm permanently damaged."*
- *"No one will want me now."*
- *"I should always be in control of my emotions."*

Black-and-white thinking reflects a fixed mindset.[1] People with a fixed mindset believe that who they are is who they will always be, so there's no reason to put in effort to change. For example, believing that you've always struggled with boundaries, so you'll continue to struggle with boundaries is reflective of a fixed mindset.

If you don't believe healing is possible, you're less likely to even try. It becomes a self-fulfilling prophecy: "I don't believe healing is possible for me; therefore, healing won't be possible for me." As Henry Ford, the founder of Ford Motor Company, said, "Whether you think you can or you can't, you're right."

For sustainable healing to occur, you need a growth mindset,[2] which means you believe change is possible, even if you haven't seen it yet. Instead of shaming yourself for where you're at, become curious about it, considering solutions you might've missed or other ways you could make progress.

A growth mindset turns impassible roadblocks into long tunnels with a light at the end. This motivates you to keep moving forward, which makes healing possible, then probable, then inevitable.

Healing Block #4: Jumping into another relationship too soon.

When you're in pain, you want the pain to stop. So, if you're missing someone, you might think that starting a new relationship will ease your hurt. Although being single for a time is recommended for anyone who's had a recent breakup, it's non-negotiable when you've been with a narcissist.

After a narcissistic breakup, jumping into another relationship too soon is like trying to sail with a broken compass. By chance, you *might* end up somewhere nice, but more than likely, you'll end up even more lost and confused than when you started.

Think about what narcissistic abuse puts you through—love bombing, devaluing, discarding, and perhaps hoovering sends your nervous system into an uproar. Up feels down, and down feels up.

You feel like you've lost yourself. Your self-esteem is fragile, your heart is fractured, and your mind is frantic and numb all at the same time. This isn't a place from which to make healthy relationship choices.

If you jump into another relationship too soon, your focus (even subconsciously) will be on what you *don't* want. You'll think things like, *"I don't want a cheater,"* *"I don't want someone who's overbearing,"* or *"I don't want to feel dismissed or devalued."*

While these are certainly good things to *not* want, being motivated by them usually means you want the complete opposite. So, you'll look for someone whose *personality* or *presence* is very different from your narcissistic ex. This leaves you vulnerable to overlooking other concerning qualities because, *on the surface,* this person looks different from the narcissist.

Your next relationship decision shouldn't be impacted by what you want to *avoid* but by what you want to *gain.* Healthy relationship choices originate from what you do want, like loyalty, honesty, consistency, and respect.

As a general rule, a year is an effective amount of time to be single and focus on your healing and growth. Within a year's time, you'll have experienced all the holidays, seasons, and emotionally triggering dates and anniversaries. You'll have invested a significant amount of time in understanding narcissistic abuse, recognizing a narcissist, and protecting yourself from toxic people.

And most importantly, you'll have proven to yourself that you are capable of being self-sufficient, self-compassionate, and self-determining. You will know what you like and don't like, where your boundaries are, and the things that you can and can't compromise on.

You will be a different *you* next year. And that will make *all* the difference.

Healing Block #5: Constantly worrying that *you* are the narcissist.

Because of the intense gaslighting and blame-shifting that happens in narcissistic relationships, many people worry that *they* are the narcissist.

The biggest reason this thought is so detrimental is because it makes the narcissist's behaviors your starting point. If you *intensely* don't want to be a narcissist, then you'll avoid anything that could *possibly* be perceived as narcissistic. This all-or-nothing thinking is where bad choices start.

For example, many of my clients (especially those raised by narcissistic parents) have such a fear of being selfish or inconsiderate that they feel immense guilt for doing *anything* for themselves.

They ruminate about if what they said was too harsh, the boundary was too firm, or the time off was too much. It's as if they have an external critical voice looking down on them, judging everything they do, and constantly labeling their behaviors as *narcissistic* or *not narcissistic*.

You don't need to let narcissism be your standard. Focus on being kind, empathetic, and respectful while also being consistent, honest, and grounded. Set boundaries and be authentic. If you expect the same consistent, kind treatment from others as you expect from yourself, then you will be far from narcissistic.

Healing Block #6: Believing you should've known better.

In the right circumstances, anyone can fall for a narcissist's manipulations. And those who say, "I would never fall for that," or "I could never be that naïve," are at greatest risk.

Most narcissists remain narcissists because it works for them. They get what they want: narcissistic supply, validation, a sense of superiority, and a feeling of control.

And to get those things, they must reel you in. The mask must be convincing; otherwise, there would be no illusion. There would be no narcissistic cycle of abuse without the love bombing phase. There would be no trauma bond if there were no *good days*.

Narcissists are expert manipulators because their profession is acting like someone they're not.

Let's break this down for a moment. What sounds crazier: to believe that someone is who they say or to believe that they're secretly gaslighting you to undermine your sense of self because they need constant validation and reassurance to soothe their own pathological insecurities?

The latter is the truth—but what kind of person without an understanding of narcissism would think that?

What narcissists do is so crazy that you feel crazy for even explaining it. But you're not crazy. You're a rational person looking for reasonable explanations for irrational behaviors.

As a society, we're also *primed* to believe in narcissists. The underlying message in every fairytale is that even the worst relationships can have happy endings. All you need to do is persevere through the bad, then surely, good will come. The beast becomes a prince, bad guys become good, and even villains can be saved with enough time, patience, and love.

And in the movies, the villains that *can't* be saved—are *always bad*. These are the villains that are portrayed as scary, unpleasant, or unattractive. In fairytales, truly harmful people are always bad.

But in the real world, the villains have some "good days" and look like the heroes: charming, flattering, unassuming, sweet, attractive, and benevolent.

The truth is some people don't *want* to be good. Some people don't *want* to change. Some people understand what they're doing is wrong … *they just don't care.*

Feeling like you should've known better is like blaming yourself for walking into someone else's bear trap. You didn't know it was there. You didn't intend to get trapped or hurt. Don't take responsibility for what the *narcissist* did. Don't hold yourself accountable for what you didn't know. The only thing that matters is what you do with what you know *now*.

Healing Block #7: Believing the narcissist targeted you because you're weak.

After narcissistic abuse, it's common to ask yourself, *"How did I fall for this?" "What's wrong with me?"* or *"Why didn't I see the red flags?"*

Most (if not all) of my clients struggle with these questions. You wonder why the narcissist chose you, and you feel foolish for ever having believed them.

But narcissists don't look for the weak—they look for the strong. They look for those who are everything they're not:

- Empathetic
- Loyal
- Honest

- Authentic

- Compassionate

- Consistent

- Self-Reflective

You weren't targeted because of everything that was "wrong" with you; you were targeted because of everything that was *right* with you!

Everything you did was an attempt to make a wrong situation, right; an illogical situation, sane; a harmful situation, healed. You sought truth in the lies, light in the darkness, and hope in the chaos.

You were being loyal, committed, and compassionate. You weren't being stupid or weak-minded. You reflected on the issues and sought meaningful solutions.

You aren't the problem. This wasn't your fault. You didn't deserve this.

The only thing you need to do is accept and own your beautiful qualities and protect them with healthy boundaries. Because once you recognize who you *really* are—the narcissist doesn't stand a chance.

Narcissists manipulate you the most when you don't see your worth. Acknowledging and owning who you are not only empowers you but keeps the narcissists at bay, too.

Healing Block #8: Thinking that you must decide whether to stay or go right now.

If you're still in a narcissistic relationship, you might be vacillating between whether you should stay or go. If you've been thinking about this for weeks, months, or years and still haven't decided, it's okay to *decide not to decide*. The right choices rarely, if ever, originate from anxiety.

Give yourself time to follow through on the healing process outlined in this book. Invest in other areas of your life that make you feel stronger and more confident, capable, and competent.

Determine to check in with yourself a month from now, three months from now, and six months from now, to see if your decision feels any clearer. Creating a checkpoint gives structure to the chaos.

If you spend all your mental and emotional energy obsessing, ruminating, and worrying about what you should do regarding the relationship, you won't have anything left to devote to healing.

Sometimes it's not about making a decision; sometimes, it's about becoming a healthier you.

And once you become a healthier you, the indecisiveness rolls away. If you were trapped in quicksand and needed to get to a boat to escape, your first task would be to get out of the quicksand, not map a route to the boat.

Save yourself first, then find your way to the boat.

Healing Block #9: Believing you need their apology to heal.

Do you ever think, *"If they would just acknowledge what they did to me, then I could move on?"*

Wanting recognition of your pain is normal. As your awareness of the hurt increases, so does your desire for it to be seen and appreciated. If the narcissist would apologize, you believe you could heal faster and easier.

At least if they acknowledged what they did, you would no longer wonder if you're just being "sensitive," "crazy," or "overdramatic." If they admitted that they lied, manipulated, gaslighted, and used you, then you could sink into your chair with a heavy but vindicated sigh and say to yourself, *"I knew it."*

And that's exactly it—the part of you that feels like you *need* their apology to heal is the same part of you that doubts your experiences. The more you self-gaslight, the more you feel like you need the narcissist's apology to get closure.

They had the power to harm you; they don't have the power to heal you. Healing is not for narcissists to give; it is a gift you give yourself.

Believing that you need them to validate your pain is a continuation of the narcissist's psychological control. They acted like they knew everything, had all the answers, and had ultimate say in what's true for you—but they don't.

No one knows what you've been through better than you. And the more you grow in self-trust, the less significant their voice becomes. Don't make your healing contingent on their apology.

You don't need them to admit their faults to feel their effects, and you don't need them to acknowledge your pain to make it real.

WRAPPING UP HEALING BLOCKS

Now that you're familiar with the most common blocks to healing, take a moment to review this chapter and see which ones resonate with you. Knowing which healing blocks you're most susceptible to can be a huge help in this process.

It's the difference between wondering, *"Why can't I get over this?"* and knowing, *"I get why I'm struggling with this—I can give myself more grace and time in this area."*

The next chapter shows you how to give your pain a purpose. And that path is paved by *post-traumatic growth.*

CHAPTER THIRTEEN

Post-Traumatic Growth: The Path to Lasting Freedom

"To anyone struggling or thinking they'll never get out of this, you're not alone. Every day is another chance to change the ending of your story. It's never too late."
–Naomi

Narcissistic abuse shakes you to your core. It makes you reevaluate everything you thought you knew about yourself, people, and the world. And that's because trauma is a "disruption of core belief systems."[1] It triggers a cascade of inner chaos, confusion, and transition. Everything seems senseless, pointless, and purposeless.

And *that* is the crux of healing: making meaning out of something that seems so senseless. You have to decide what you're going to do with what you've endured.

What purpose will this pain serve? How will you think, feel, and act differently now that you're aware of narcissists and the harm of narcissistic abuse?

Wishing that these things never happened is unquestionably valid, and there must be a period of grieving. But sometimes, our most painful moments lead to our biggest transformations.

When you're faced with situations that challenge your most deeply held beliefs (e.g., "Everyone deserves a second chance," "It's selfish of me to set boundaries.") you're forced to see things in a new light. We tend to believe what we're taught until those beliefs hit a wall.

And for many of us, narcissists are that wall. They make you rethink your beliefs about how to make a relationship work, the best ways to communicate, and who you are as a person.

It's not uncommon to experience symptoms of post-traumatic stress disorder (PTSD) in response to narcissistic abuse.[2] Recognizing these PTSD symptoms and exploring whether complex post-traumatic stress disorder (CPTSD) could provide an even more accurate description of your symptoms is part of the healing process.

And once healing is underway, there's also another possible response: post-traumatic *growth*. Post-traumatic growth refers to the positive change people experience after tragedies, adversities, or traumatic events.[3] Post-traumatic growth happens when you take what you thought you knew, mix it with what you now know, and emerge with an even deeper sense of authenticity, purpose, and fortitude.

The following sections will help you recognize ways you've already grown and provide mindset shifts and practical strategies for post-traumatic growth in five areas[4]: appreciation for life, relationships with others, new possibilities, personal strength, and spirituality.

I've also included encouraging words from other survivors. Their statements are in response to the question, *"What advice would you give to someone who is looking to heal from narcissistic abuse?"*

What they shared is profound, insightful, and meant *just for you.*

APPRECIATION FOR LIFE

Notice the Good in the World

"The best disinfectant is sunlight ... Tell people you know you can trust and will be a support to you ... Read the books and educate yourself. When you learn what you are dealing with, it empowers you. You aren't crazy, you are worthy, and you do deserve better."
—Michelle

Narcissists are like solar eclipses—they block the sun until you forget the light exists. But just like solar eclipses don't last forever, the narcissist's shadow doesn't have to cast darkness on your world forever, either.

There is still *good* in the world, even if you have to look for it a little harder right now. Find movies you can laugh at, pets you can cherish, and moments of contentment. Notice the innocence of a baby and the pure joy of a child's laugh. Watch the leaves sway uncaringly in the breeze, and the birds soar on the wings of the wind.

Notice the consistency of the world around you—the sun rises and sets, the stars twinkle, and the moon beams. As Albus Dumbledore remarked in J.K. Rowling's famous *Harry Potter* series, "Happiness can be found, even in the darkest of times, if one only remembers to turn on the light."

Keeping with the *Harry Potter* theme for a moment, narcissists are much like dementors, those dark creatures that make you feel as if you'll never be happy again. In the wizarding world, the only way to fight the dementors is by conjuring a Patronus charm—a spell that can only be evoked by intense concentration on your *happiest memories* or *most treasured relationships*. Dementors are repulsed by the depth of your unconditional love and heartwarming memories because they can only control you if you become overwhelmed by sadness, hopelessness, and anguish.

Narcissists are much the same way. The happier and healthier you get, the less the narcissist can control you. That's why they work so hard to make you look *only* at them. Be intentional to widen your view beyond the narcissist.

Increase Intentional Gratitude

"You are worth saving. Do not give up. It is not your fault. God
loves you."
–Kristen

Gratitude is a change in perspective. It's being in the same room but standing on the opposite side. It's seeing the ways you show up for yourself. It's noticing that you didn't get as triggered today as you did yesterday. It's appreciating your strengths even if the narcissist fails to see them.

Narcissistic relationships take up so much of your valuable time and energy. But narcissists don't deserve those precious commodities. Time and energy only flow in one direction. You can't get them back once they're gone.

You are the gatekeeper to your time and energy. You can't be everything to everyone. And you will end up feeling empty if you try.

There will always be good and bad in the world. There will always be hurt, abuse, and cruelty, and there will always be kindness, goodness, and selflessness. Gratitude isn't about making the best of things or looking for good in a bad situation. It's about finding the things that are *good* and being grateful for them.

Waking up, being able to walk, having a job, driving a car, and sleeping in a bed are all *good things* to be grateful for. It doesn't mean that you don't have difficult situations. But it does mean you don't overlook the good because you're staring at the bad.

Reassess Your Priorities

"Be kind to yourself and don't beat yourself up ... Love yourself, take care of yourself, read a lot, and stay busy doing the things you love. Seek help from a certified therapist or someone who understands narcissistic abuse. Join a support group, and again, be gentle on yourself. Your heart was broken, and it will heal."
—Robin

Nothing puts things in perspective like a crisis. Trauma leaves you with no choice but to prioritize what is truly important. Self-care can no longer wait when you're bleeding out. When you experience something that shocks your system, you have to reevaluate how you're living your life and why.

Narcissistic relationships have a way of dominating your mental and emotional resources. You end up investing ninety percent of your emotional energy into toxic relationships, which leaves ten percent for the healthy ones. This imbalance isn't sustainable or fair. Healthy people deserve more of your time than toxic ones.

Use this insight to reassess your priorities. Think about what *really* matters to you in life. How much value are you placing on the narcissist's requests? Do you want the opinions of others to dictate who you are and how you spend your time? Is worrying about the future really making it better? Are you living your life in a way you can look back on and be proud of? At the end of the day, you are the only one who can answer these questions for *you*.

RELATIONSHIPS WITH OTHERS

Find a Sense of Belonging

"You matter. What you have gone through is confusing, but it is also real. It makes sense that you need to heal because you have truly been hurt, invalidated, and silenced. But your voice matters, and healing is possible. You are not alone."
—Anonymous

When you're rejected, you're forced to see where you will be accepted. Narcissists are masterful at making you feel like you have no home, no place to go, and nowhere to belong. And although at first, they might succeed in making you feel this way, they can't keep you there.

Because what narcissists don't realize is that their attempts to *displace* you paradoxically create a space *for* you. When a narcissist consistently devalues or discards you, you join the (conservatively calculated) *ninety-nine million people* who've endured narcissistic abuse. And just like that, you have millions of people who can relate to what you're going through.

Search out narcissistic abuse support groups or even related groups like those for bereavement, emotional abuse, or betrayal trauma. Open up conversations with those around you to see who else might be experiencing difficult, toxic, or painful relationships. Even following narcissistic abuse survivor pages on social media can help increase your sense of belonging. If you'd like to join my community, you can do so at https://www.chelseybrookecole.com/contact or scan the QR code.

After experiencing narcissistic relationships, your capacity to appreciate healthy relationships deepens. Because if you've only had relatively healthy relationships, you *expect* people to be honest and loyal. You take for granted that people will tell the truth, be reasonable, and not intentionally hurt you.

But after you've been with a narcissist, you realize none of those things are a given. You stop assuming people will follow through and, instead, wait and watch. So, when someone is genuinely authentic, compassionate, and committed, you feel an appreciation for them on a whole new level.

Your friend's loyalty means so much more. Your new partner's kindness means so much more. Your sister's phone calls mean so much more. And this profound sense of gratitude for people being who they say they are leads to stronger, more meaningful relationships.

Notice the Ways Your Empathy has Grown

"Be patient and kind to yourself; you cannot and will not heal overnight. It will take many forms of help and recovery ... Speak good things into your life and about yourself. You will have better days, just have faith and trust the process. You have a bigger purpose for surviving through what you did, so give yourself a chance to heal and help others with what you've learned. If you can be an ally to someone that needs it, then please do it. Narc survivors

*often feel lonely and abandoned, and we need to be there for one
another."*
–Nia

I know many of you feel like the last thing you need to be is *more*
empathetic. But your empathy is a gift—it's only in not knowing how
to protect it that you get hurt.

Although narcissistic abuse might cause you to dampen or shrink your
empathy for a time, overall, it *increases* your capacity for empathy.
Now, you can empathize with people in ways you couldn't before
because *you've been there.*

Narcissists think they're hurting you. And no doubt, they do. But they
also open your eyes to the world of toxic people that perhaps you
didn't see before. You're wiser, more perceptive, and more
knowledgeable now than you were. What they meant for your harm,
you can use for good.

You can take your pain and hold it up to someone else's pain to say,
"Me too." You can hold back on judging someone's decision to stay
because you know it's not always easy to leave.

You can recognize someone's subtle attempts to hide their emotional
bruises because you tried to hide them before, too. You can listen to
someone's story without trying to fix it because you know how
painful it is to not feel heard. You can take everything you've endured
and use it in a way to see, understand, and help others more sincerely,
intimately, and passionately—*because* of what you've been through.

NEW POSSIBILITIES

Recognize Your Adaptability

"Some people may not understand why we stay for so long. It isn't your fault. You tried. You can't heal people who don't want to heal. You can only be in charge of yourself and protect and love yourself ... You are perfect the way you are inside and out. Please remember to be kind to yourself because you owe that much to yourself ... Some days are harder than others, but you will get through this. I promise, one day, you'll wake up and take a deep breath, and it'll feel a little less heavy. You are strong, stronger than you may believe. You've lived through this, so you can get through anything!"
–Baileah

Was there ever a moment during your narcissistic relationship when you thought, *"I can't keep doing this,"* or *"Something has to change"?*

Oftentimes, we don't alter our way of doing things until we feel like we have no other choice. And when you experience narcissistic abuse, you're hit with the hard reality that there are some things you can't do.

You can't change someone, no matter how much you want to. You can't do enough to make some people happy. You can't solve a relationship problem if the other person wants to keep the problem. You can only go so far until you can't go any further.

At first, this truth feels like a lose-lose situation. Your current communication strategies don't work. Your ideas on how to have a successful relationship don't work. Ultimately, nothing works.

This leaves you feeling as if you're floating in space with nothing to ground you. But it's this highly uncomfortable experience that serves as the catalyst for post-traumatic growth.

Out of necessity for your own sanity, you explore other possibilities. You wonder: *"What if this isn't me?" "What if I can't change this?" "What can I do?"* When you're hurting, you need answers. You need to understand how someone you love could hurt you so much. You need to know why nothing works with this person.

And that's how trauma spurs new interests and compels you to investigate things you wouldn't have otherwise. You learn to adapt, think differently, and find creative solutions. You realize that healthy communication strategies backfire when dealing with a toxic person. By looking into new areas, you grow, evolve, and understand more.

When looking at where you are now, appreciate how far you've come. What do you understand or realize now that you didn't six months ago? A year ago? How much more do you understand not only about narcissism but also about how to set boundaries or listen to your intuition?

Change can be painful, especially change you didn't ask for. But you get to decide how this change will impact you going forward.

PERSONAL STRENGTH

Acknowledge Your Resilience and Self-Reliance

"Remember that you were targeted BECAUSE of your amazing qualities. You are not weak or crazy, or unlovable. You are amazing, and that's why this type of person needed you in their life. They saw in you all the strength, care, and empathy they were never capable of possessing. And trust the wisdom of your body. It will never lie to

you. That feeling of anxiety or uneasiness is a messenger. You are not paranoid or crazy; you are intuitive and insightful. Trust yourself."
–Lena

Effectively dealing with trauma means updating your beliefs based on your new experiences. Now you recognize that some people act in cruel ways not because they don't understand but because they don't care. You recognize that some people would rather weaponize your empathy than appreciate it. You recognize that some people want to twist and distort your reality to control you.

And this recognition leaves you with two choices: give up your voice or fight for it. Once you see that someone is gaslighting you, you must cling to your reality with everything you have because you might be the *only one* who sees it.

Although this can feel like stubbornness at first, it's actually resilience. You learn to trust what *you* see, hear, and feel instead of accepting what you're told to believe.

You are resilient in ways you probably don't even realize. When you disengage from the narcissist's triggering comments, find humor in how ridiculous their accusations are, and use coping skills even on days you don't feel like it, you're being resilient.

Take a moment to write out all the ways you've tried to deal with or heal from narcissistic abuse. The point isn't to critique your healing. The point is to see how much you've invested in developing, progressing, and evolving. This is *proof* of your resilience.

Self-reliance and self-sufficiency aren't born out of having plenty; they're born out of having nothing. When you feel like you have nothing left to give—when your emotional reserves are empty, and your heart is crushed—you get a chance to see what you're truly capable of.

You might not feel like you're there yet but keep this quote by Dr. Najwa Zebian in mind: "Broken wings are a sign of struggle. And strength."

Paint Your Personal Narrative

"Share and understand that you are not what the narcissist pulled you down to be. Find your authentic self, find a way to begin to let go of the labels and hurt someone else has burdened you with ... Trust your instincts ... forgive yourself for something you couldn't see coming. And when they say that they 'made you into the person you are today,' give them credit for causing the pain that brought on the will to change."
—Anonymous

Imagine an abstract canvas that's painted only in colors of black, white, and gray. It might have an interesting design, pattern, or theme, but overall, it is plain, ordinary, and muted. Now, imagine splashes of vibrant colors being added to the canvas.

Where there was just black and white, now there are whisps of coral reds, pastel pinks, and hints of soft orange, falling together like a sunset. Where there was only gray, now there are hues of blues and greens, colliding together like ocean waves.

Which canvas displays more depth and keeps your gaze longer? Naturally, the one with more colors.

Your life is a canvas. The things that go as planned are represented in black and white. They provide a solid background, stability, and consistency.

But the unexpected things—which usually include the beautiful moments and the hurts, traumas, and letdowns—are represented in color. They stand out in bold and become imprinted in your mind as moments you'll never forget.

The more difficulties someone has faced, the more interesting we think they are. We give our time and money to listen to speakers who overcame seemingly insurmountable odds. We're inspired by those who live without things we take for granted every day.

The hurts of life leave scars, but scars tell stories. And you get to decide how your story will be told. What will you make your experiences of narcissistic abuse *mean* about *you*?

Will you decide to believe, *"I'm worthless, and that's why I suffered this abuse,"* or will you affirm, *"I'm a survivor, which reflects my strength and resilience"*?

You get to decide, you know. The narcissists in your life want you to believe that you don't have a choice. But that's a lie. You do have a choice—always have and always will.

Kintsugi[5] is a centuries-old Japanese art form focused on mending broken pottery with liquid or powdered gold. While you might be tempted to view broken pottery as irreparable, the kintsugi philosophy provides a healthier alternative: things that are broken aren't meant to be discarded; they're meant to be remade.

You might feel like a broken vase that's shattered on the floor. But you can be put back together, piece by piece until the latter is more intricate and beautiful than the former.

Highlight the edges of your broken pieces with gold. Be proud of the way you reconstructed yourself. You are deliberately and intentionally building a version of you that is more authentic, experienced, and mature. You aren't beyond repair; you're being redesigned.

SPIRITUALITY

Create a Deeper Faith or Life Philosophy

"I had to remember who I was before the abuse: a young, naïve girl. I had to go back there ... in other words, I had to remind myself this was not my fault, that I have value as a human being, that I am loved and still capable of loving others in a healthy way. His abuse does not define my self-worth."
—Kristen

Narcissistic abuse sends you into an existential crisis:

- "What does it all mean?"

- "What's my purpose?"

- "Why do bad things happen to good people?"

- "What good can come out of this?"

- "How do you move forward after enduring unnecessary and senseless heartache?"

- "Why did this happen to me? Am I being punished for something?"

- "Maybe I deserve this because of my past mistakes."

This crisis sends you on the hunt for answers and understanding. You try to make sense of not only how or why this happened to you but why someone would be so cruel in the first place. You question your faith in humanity, your belief in people's goodness, and the fairness of life.

The injustices of these relationships can cause you to question your convictions, spirituality, and religious beliefs. The way narcissists are so often successful, well-liked, and live without consequence despite all the harm they cause evokes a very disturbing, gut-wrenching feeling. You wonder if there's any order to life at all or if everything is futile.

Grappling with these questions is a very real part of the healing journey. When everything you thought you knew about life and love gets obliterated, it's normal to wonder what's true.

For some, narcissistic abuse leads them to trust no one and view humanity as selfish, greedy, and callous. For others, narcissistic abuse deepens and strengthens their religious beliefs as they have hope for ultimate justice, believing that everyone will be held accountable for their actions in the end.

For post-traumatic growth to occur, it's important to spend time with these questions and come to a resolution that feels true for you and the person you want to be. If you rush this process, it's typical to develop a suspicious or pessimistic outlook on life.

And while it's not uncommon to have that initially, an enduring pessimistic worldview has negative effects, including a higher risk for depression and anxiety disorders, as well as low resilience and distress tolerance.[6] If you feel like you're stuck in a pessimistic viewpoint, therapy and healthy supports are recommended, as this could indicate a chronic trauma response.

Reevaluating, exploring, and deepening your religious or spiritual beliefs is important for your healing, as it's one of the pillars of post-traumatic growth.[7] As human beings, we want to believe that our pain had a purpose. It's one of the ways we cope with the injustices of the world.

Essentially all religions and cultures provide a framework for universal truths: there is good and bad, right and wrong, light and dark, and evil and morality. Framing narcissistic abuse as one of many bad things that exist in the world makes it less personal.

It's not that the universe chose to punish you; it's that bad people do bad things. You didn't deserve it, it shouldn't have happened, and it's not your fault.

In this imperfect world, sometimes good people get hurt. Is this a good enough reason for you to give up on love, hope, and faith altogether? Only you can answer that for yourself.

But before you come to a conclusion, consider this: *"How much control do you want the narcissist to have in your life?"*

If narcissists are the reason you stop having faith in people or seeing anything good in the world, then even if they aren't physically in your life anymore, their shadow remains. And that shadow can cast darkness on every part of your life.

Most religions speak about karma, payback, righteous judgment, or checks and balances. Although we usually mistakenly make this mean, "bad things shouldn't happen to good people," there's another way to understand this: time catches up with all of us. No one can outrun their bad choices forever (not even narcissists).

But perhaps even more importantly—when you lie down at night or take your last breath, what do you want to see? Will the narcissist(s) who hurt you be your last thought?

Or do you want to see the good moments you had despite the pain? Do you want to feel hate and disdain for the narcissist, or do you want to feel proud of the person you've become? In the grand scheme of your life, how much room do you want the narcissist to take up?

Coming to terms with these thoughts will help you tremendously in resolving your existential crisis and deepening your faith and spiritual beliefs.

And if, right now, these existential questions feel too heavy, messy, or irrelevant, that's okay. Take your time through the rest of the healing journey and come back to this section when you're ready to see it with an open heart.

Find Meaning and Purpose

"I am proof that it's possible to move from being a scared, compliant, people pleaser who has no idea of her rights or how to handle those who abuse and take advantage of her into someone who can recognize a toxic individual and steer clear or cut them out completely from my life. To be able to create boundaries to protect myself from those who delight in hurting others. To be happy in loving relationships, enjoying healthy and peaceful relationships. No longer a people pleaser (although I still do sometimes) but understanding that not worrying about what other people think is how I become the real me."
–Lillee

Narcissists make you feel like you don't matter—that your efforts are pointless, your goals are unattainable, and your hopes are futile. Giving back is one way you take your power back.

This can be done in small and big ways, but the end goal is the same: creating a sense of meaning and significance. Helping others or getting involved in personally meaningful causes gives you reason to believe that *you do matter*.

You can write books, stories, or poetry, compose music, start a support group, bring awareness to narcissistic abuse in your church or community, or join an organization whose mission you resonate with.

Because narcissism is the opposite of authenticity, being around narcissists makes you realize how important it is to be real, genuine, and reliable. While they focus on selfish gain, you focus on selfless giving. While they make excuses for all their mistakes, you hold yourself and others to the same standard.

Knowing who you are not only helps you survive narcissistic abuse, but it separates you from their control. Use your life experiences to live with more intention, consistency, and purpose.

Acknowledge Your Greater Level of Awareness

"Always know that it's never too late to heal and have a healthy life."
–Robin

Who would you trust more to help you build wealth: someone who was born into a wealthy family or someone who was born into poverty but became wealthy over time?

We naturally give more credibility to those who have experienced obstacles and succeeded. In every area of life, we give more weight to those who have the background, education, or experiences to back up what they think.

And yet, as a narcissistic abuse survivor, there's a tendency to view what you've been through as indicative of weakness, ineptitude, or personal failure.

But these experiences should be viewed as life lessons that give you *more* credibility, legitimacy, and influence. *You know* what a toxic relationship is like. *You know* what it feels like to be gaslighted. *You know* how strong a trauma bond can be. And *you know* how much effort, energy, and strength it takes to heal from toxic relationships.

Who should someone trust more with their relationship questions: a person who's only ever had healthy interactions or a person who's had healthy and toxic ones?

While I know some of you might feel like you've only ever had toxic or unhealthy relationships, give it time. Your commitment to healing will ensure that you create healthy ones in the future or strengthen the ones you already have.

But one thing's for sure: no one can take away the lessons you learned while being in a toxic relationship.

You are more equipped now than ever to help someone set healthy boundaries because you know how dangerous it is not to. You are more equipped now than ever to help someone identify red flags because you know how painful it is to ignore them. You are more equipped now than ever to teach the importance of self-compassion, trusting your intuition, and speaking the truth because you know that *not* doing so is an open door for narcissists and toxic people of all kinds.

Your views, opinions, and insights are more credible and valid now than ever *because* of what you've been through. Never believe you can't make healthy choices—you are far more qualified than you realize.

If this realization hasn't happened yet, give it time. One day, you'll be talking to someone about a relationship issue, and they'll say something like, "Well, I don't think anyone *intentionally* hurts someone," or "I think most relationship issues are due to miscommunication," … and it'll hit you like a ton of bricks: *they don't get it*. They don't know what a narcissist is like. They have no idea how much danger they're in.

And in that moment, you'll realize how far you've come, how much you've learned, and how empowered you are. And a feeling will bubble up inside of you that wants to save them and tell them everything that happened to you in the hopes that they will learn how to protect themselves.

And some people will be open to your words and take them to heart, while others will categorize you as being cynical, hypervigilant, overdramatic, or ridiculous so they can maintain their worldview that everyone means well.

But how they view you doesn't really matter. Because *you know* what you've been through. And so do the millions of other narcissistic abuse survivors on this journey toward healing, recovery, and empowerment.

You are never alone. You always have a safe space. Welcome to the place you belong—*we're all here with you.*

A PERSONAL NOTE TO YOU

First, I want to say *thank you*. Thank you for taking the time to read this book. For opening your heart and trusting me to guide you. For giving me your precious time and energy. You could've read any book (and I hope you read many more!). But I'm truly honored and grateful that you read mine.

Second, I want you to reflect on the journey you've just been through. How are you feeling? What insights or "ah ha" moments did you experience? We covered a lot of content on narcissists, understanding your upbringing, and post-traumatic growth.

I divided this book into three parts to give you a full-circle picture of healing. You need all three pieces to fully appreciate what you've been through with the narcissist, how your specific childhood impacted you, and what you need for long-lasting growth. These topics often evoke a lot of emotions, so give yourself space to talk and journal about your realizations.

Finally, if you're interested in working with me through therapy or coaching or looking for more healing opportunities, online courses, extra support, or any of the free downloads mentioned in this book, please visit my website at https://www.chelseybrookecole.com or scan the QR code.

Again, *thank you* for allowing me to be a part of your healing journey and please reach out if you'd like to connect or share your story!

With all my appreciation,

Chelsey

WHAT CLIENTS AND READERS SAY ABOUT CHELSEY

"For anyone reading this, I went through one of the worst experiences in my life with a partner who not only exhibited traits of narcissism, but also BPD, HPD, and bipolar. Chelsey helped me more in a two-hour time block after she got to know my situation than anyone else or anything else I was doing. I'm alive, at a place of indifference, and doing well because of things I learned through working with her. Chelsey, thank you for everything!" –Michael

"I am very grateful to be working with Chelsey. I have had experiences of working with other practitioners where they did not thoroughly comprehend the dynamics and impact of narcissistic abuse. I had to actually explain in-depth many experiences and it was retraumatizing. Working with Chelsey helps because she is so kind and understanding and deeply informed, and she truly meets you at the level you are at." –Robert

"Chelsey helped me through a very difficult time in my life when a narcissist pulled their mask off and tried to smear campaign me in ways I would have never expected. She was able to help me put things into perspective and confirmed my intuition was correct the entire time. It was very difficult to comprehend and understand what happened to me, having never dealt with anything like that before. I'm forever grateful for her believing in me and my side even when professionals across the board did not. It was one of, if not the worst, things I've ever been through. I felt completely isolated and alone until I met Chelsey. Thank you, Chelsey. Not only did you help me then, but knowing what I know now, that will never happen to me again. It's almost impossible for anyone to understand unless you've

lived it, and the legal system is totally flawed into believing the wrong person." –John

"Despite appearing outwardly confident, I had struggled with self-doubt and self-worth for most of my life. I was my own biggest critic and convinced myself that I was not worthy of success. I can honestly say working with Chelsey was one of the best decisions I have ever made. Chelsey was the consummate professional. She put me at ease from the start. I learnt so much from our sessions, especially about self-care, and I feel so much healthier and happier. I feel equipped, like Chelsey gave me a toolbox that I can dip into whenever I feel the need. I highly recommend Chelsey, she is not just another counselor with a paper qualification, she is the real deal, someone who knows exactly how to help you make changes, because she made them herself! Thank you, Chelsey!" –Ed

"I knew from a very early age that something wasn't right in my world. I didn't know what it was, and I didn't know what to call it. Once I found Chelsey's writings, she not only brought a light to what had been and what ultimately would be my world, she identified it. It was at this point I learned what narcissism was, could identify its traits, and I felt validated—what I was dealing with had a name. Thank you so much for bringing clarity to my world in addition to the understanding and strength to move forward in it. Your insight is truly a ray of sunshine that has touched my heart." –Sandi

"As much as I've researched and read information and finally realized who and what I'm dealing with, Chelsey is the one and only who I feel fully gets it and explains it all exactly as it really is. The experiences, the feelings, the pain ... ALL of it! It's not just research and book smart knowledge ... SHE KNOWS. It's very validating to have someone who articulates it perfectly. She fully understands and

truly wants to help others going through the absolute hell the narcissist has created and keeps you bound to. She's a 'beacon of light' in the darkness!" –Lisa

"Chelsey puts into words concisely and clearly all the abuse I went through for 20 years. She defines the truth and brings to light the reality of narcissistic abuse. The isolation this abuse brings is so damaging. Reading Chelsey's truth has given me the courage to face what I went through and talk about it." –Cassi

"I lived my entire life under the thumb of narcissists: first, my mother, then, my husband. He discarded and divorced me after 47.5 years, after I learned about narcissism and became uncooperative and much harder to manipulate. Finally being free from him, I feel like I've been let out of a cage! Reading Chelsey's posts are helping me to recognize and heal from all those years of narcissistic abuse. Thank you, Chelsey!" –Bev

"Chelsey's content has helped me to make sense of what happened to me as I continue to work through the trauma of surviving narcissistic abuse. It is so validating to have a story for every situation she describes, and it helps me with my ongoing reality testing. She really understands how narcissists work, and her information helps me to work toward a version of myself that is healed and thriving." –Krysti

RESOURCES

Crisis Resources

(U.S.) Suicide and Crisis Lifeline—www.988lifeline.org or dial 988

(U.S.) National Domestic Violence Hotline—www.thehotline.org or dial 800-799-7233

International Crisis Helplines—www.findahelpline.com

Books

The Covert Passive-Aggressive Narcissist: Recognizing the Traits and Finding Healing After Hidden Emotional and Psychological Abuse by Debbie Mirza

Out of the Fog: Moving from Confusion to Clarity After Narcissistic Abuse by Dana Morningstar

Adult Children of Emotionally Immature Parents: How to Heal from Distant, Rejecting, or Self-Involved Parents by Dr. Lindsay C. Gibson

Expectation Hangover: Overcoming Disappointment in Work, Love, and Life by Christine Hassler

No Bad Parts: Healing Trauma and Restoring Wholeness with the Internal Family Systems Model by Dr. Richard Schwartz

Will I Ever Be Good Enough? Healing the Daughters of Narcissistic Mothers by Dr. Karyl McBride

Should I Stay or Should I Go? Surviving a Relationship with a Narcissist by Dr. Ramani Durvasula

Welcome Home: A Guide to Building a Home for Your Soul by Dr. Najwa Zebian

The Body Keeps the Score: Brain, Mind, and Body in the Healing of Trauma by Dr. Bessel Van Der Kolk

13 Things Mentally Strong People Don't Do: Take Back Your Power, Embrace Change, Face Your Fears, and Train Your Brain for Happiness and Success by Amy Morin

Man's Search for Meaning by Dr. Viktor E. Frankl

Boundaries: When to Say Yes, How to Say No to Take Control of Your Life by Dr. Henry Cloud and Dr. John Townsend

Complex PTSD: From Surviving to Thriving by Pete Walker

Believing Me: Healing from Narcissistic Abuse and Complex Trauma by Dr. Ingrid Clayton

What My Bones Know: A Memoir of Healing from Complex Trauma by Stephanie Foo

Healing from Hidden Abuse: A Journey Through the Stages of Recovery from Psychological Abuse by Shannon Thomas, LCSW

Been There Got Out: Toxic Relationships, High-Conflict Divorce, and How to Stay Sane Under Insane Circumstances by Lisa Johnson and Chris Barry

The Empath's Survival Guide: Life Strategies for Sensitive People by Dr. Judith Orloff

Sensitive: The Hidden Power of the Highly Sensitive Person in a Loud, Fast, Too-Much World by Jenn Granneman and Andre Soló

The Introvert Advantage: How Quiet People Can Thrive in an Extrovert World by Dr. Marti Olsen Laney

Quiet: The Power of Introverts in a World that Can't Stop Talking by Susan Cain

For a more comprehensive resource list, please visit
https://www.chelseybrookecole.com/support-resources or scan the
QR code.

ABOUT THE AUTHOR

Growing up, I tried very hard to be "good enough." I desperately wanted to feel whole—to be seen and heard. To know that I didn't have to earn love.

Back then, I didn't have a name for what I was experiencing. I didn't realize that I can't fix a problem I'm not creating. All I knew was that I felt different, defective, and damaged.

My early relationships reflected my mindset at that time. I was used to trying to "win" someone's love. I was used to feeling like I was fundamentally flawed—that even though *other* people could have healthy relationships, the best I could do was find someone else who was broken and help them heal. Then, and only then, would I finally earn love.

This left me vulnerable to highly narcissistic people—those who saw second chances as a pass to keep hurting me. Those who took advantage of my patience, manipulated my kindness, and ignored my needs.

For over a decade, I had relationships with narcissists. I was betrayed, lied to, disregarded, and rejected. I was cheated on, smear campaigned against (still am), and called about every name you could think of. And I still have to interact with narcissists in various capacities.

Realizing that I was experiencing narcissistic abuse was a process. I felt a lot of shame, guilt, and self-judgment for being in those relationships. For not seeing the signs sooner. For ignoring my intuition and abandoning myself.

But as I healed, I learned to look at myself differently. I gave myself compassion for what I had been through. I gave myself grace for not knowing what I didn't know. I allowed myself time and space to grieve and feel all the emotions from chronic betrayal trauma.

And it's through this process of intentionally building "me" that I found my life's mission: helping people heal from narcissistic abuse.

Today, my life looks very different than it used to. I set better boundaries, listen to my gut, and take care of myself. I trust my judgment, hold space for my feelings, and am married to a man whose kindness and selflessness stitches my broken pieces back together a little more each day.

And yet, there are still days and moments when I feel "not enough." When I question my worth, feel overcome with heaviness, overthink things I've said, and wonder if I'm doing enough. I struggle to slow down, take breaks, and give myself credit. And I've learned that those moments are part of healing. I no longer view triggers as a sign of weakness—but as validation of the pain I went through.

I'm a work in progress—always will be. And that's okay. In fact, it's more than okay. Because everything I've been through and continue to experience gives me the motivation, courage, and fortitude to keep advocating for narcissistic abuse survivors. To keep speaking against narcissistic norms. To keep giving a voice to those who feel like they've lost theirs.

I'm not giving up on me—or you. And I hope this book gives you the strength to not give up on you, either.

If it's made a positive impact, would you let me know? I can't wait to hear from you!

ACKNOWLEDGEMENTS

My ultimate appreciation is to God for creating and loving me. He gave me the skills and talents I have, and I'm determined to use those for His glory. I'm forever grateful to Him for *making all things work together for good.*

To Matt, my wonderful husband, for showing me what real, unconditional love feels like. You restored my faith in humanity and belief that there are loyal, kind people in the world. You healed my heart in so many ways. I am the best version of me when I'm with you. God blessed me to have you—and I'm so glad that I do.

To Mom, for being the most selfless and giving person I know. You've helped me in more ways than I could possibly name. Thank you for never doubting me and believing in me, even when I didn't believe in myself. You've been my biggest supporter and best friend. Your support, help, and commitment made all this possible. I'll always be your sunshine.

To my clients and fellow survivors, for inspiring me every day with your resilience, kindness, and courage. This book wouldn't have been possible without your willingness to share your stories and be open and vulnerable. This book belongs to you.

REFERENCES

Chapter Two

1. Stinson, F. S., Dawson, D. A., Goldstein, R. B., Chou, S. P., Huang, B., Smith, S. M., Ruan, W. J., Pulay, A. J., Saha, T. D., Pickering, R. P., & Grant, B. F. (2008). Prevalence, correlates, disability, and comorbidity of DSM-IV narcissistic personality disorder: Results from the wave 2 national epidemiologic survey on alcohol and related conditions. *The Journal of Clinical Psychiatry, 69*(7), 1033-1045. https://doi.org/10.4088/jcp.v69n0701

2. American Psychological Association (n.d.). Sadism. In *APA dictionary of psychology*. Retrieved January 12, 2023, from https://dictionary.apa.org/sadism

3. Dictionary (n.d.). Malevolent. In *Dictionary.com*. Retrieved January 11, 2023, from https://www.dictionary.com/browse/malevolent

4. WebMD Editorial Contributors. (2023, March 30). *Narcissism: Symptoms and signs.* https://www.webmd.com/mental-health/narcissism-symptoms-signs

5. Caligor, E., Levy, K. N., Yeomans, F. E. (2015) Narcissistic personality disorder: Diagnostic and clinical challenges. *The American Journal of Psychiatry, 172*(5), 415-422. https://doi.org/10.1176/appi.ajp.2014.14060723

6. Rice, T.R., & Hoffman, L. (2014). Defense mechanisms and implicit emotion regulation: A comparison of a psychodynamic construct with one from contemporary neuroscience. *Journal of the American Psychoanalytic Association, 62*(4). 693–708. https://doi.org/10.1177/0003065114546746

Chapter Three

1. Foster, McCain, J. L., Hibberts, M. F., Brunell, A. B., & Burke Johnson, R. (2015). The grandiose narcissism scale: A global and facet-level measure of grandiose narcissism. *Personality and Individual Differences, 73*, 12–16. https://doi.org/10.1016/j.paid.2014.08.042

2. Pincus, A. L., Cain, N. M., & Wright, A. G. (2014). Narcissistic grandiosity and narcissistic vulnerability in psychotherapy. *Personality Disorders, 5*(4), 439–443. https://doi.org/10.1037/per0000031

3. Doctor Ramani. (2021, December 21). *The self-righteous narcissist* [Video]. YouTube. https://www.youtube.com/watch?v=Ei-sy07mSbI

4. Doctor Ramani. (2020, May 25). *Neglectful narcissists: Everything you need to know (part 1/3)*. [Video]. YouTube. https://www.youtube.com/watch?v=uhYe5SuVIKc

5. Fennimore, A. K. (2021). Duplicitous me: Communal narcissists and public service motivation. *Public Personnel Management, 50*(1), 25–55. https://doi.org/10.1177/0091026019900355

6. Deveze-Villarreal, & López-Acevo, C. A. (2022). Malignant narcissism: A case report and literature review. *Medicina Universitaria, 24*(2). https://doi.org/10.24875/RMU.21000075

7. Paulhus, D. L., & Williams, K. M. (2002). The dark triad of personality: Narcissism, machiavellianism and psychopathy. *Journal of Research in Personality, 36*(6), 556–563. https://doi.org/10.1016/S0092-6566(02)00505-6

Chapter Four

1. Gupta, S. (2022, August 15). *What is the narcissistic abuse cycle?* Verywell Mind. https://www.verywellmind.com/narcissistic-abuse-cycle-stages-impact-and-coping-6363187

2. Doctor Ramani. (2020, April 10). *When narcissists "devalue" and "discard" (Glossary of narcissistic relationships)*. [Video]. YouTube. https://www.youtube.com/watch?v=Oik4IsgQ4uk&t=260s

Chapter Five

1. Doctor Ramani. (2021, December 10). *The undetectable way vulnerable narcissists love bomb*. [Video]. YouTube. https://www.youtube.com/watch?v=WctDnZQ8JVQ

2. Doctor Ramani. (2022, January 16). *Lovebombed by a self-righteous narcissist*. [Video]. YouTube. https://www.youtube.com/watch?v=AAOrklLL-C4

3. Doctor Ramani. (2021, December 29). *Have you been lovebombed by a communal narcissist?* [Video]. YouTube. https://www.youtube.com/watch?v=mFYYiCIQvOw

4. Doctor Ramani. (2021, November 26). *When malignant narcissists lovebomb*. [Video]. YouTube. https://www.youtube.com/watch?v=UmP-FoTTRn0&t=482s

5. Doctor Ramani. (2022, January 23). *Lovebombed by a neglectful narcissist*. [Video]. YouTube. https://www.youtube.com/watch?v=G6iTVcdtpVM

Chapter Six

1. Howard, V. (2019). Recognising narcissistic abuse and the implications for mental health nursing practice. *Issues in Mental Health Nursing, 40*(8), 644-654. https://doi.org/10.1080/01612840.2019.1590485

2. MedCircle. (2020, November 10). *Narcissistic abuse: What it looks like and what to do*. https://medcircle.com/articles/narcissistic-abuse/

3. Sweet, P. L. (2019). The sociology of gaslighting. *American Sociological Review, 84*(5), 851–875. https://www.jstor.org/stable/48602118

4. American Psychological Association (n.d.). Manipulation. In *APA dictionary of psychology*. Retrieved January 20, 2023, from https://dictionary.apa.org/manipulation

5. American Psychological Association (n.d.). Triangulation. In *APA dictionary of psychology*. Retrieved January 18, 2023, from https://dictionary.apa.org/triangulation

6. American Psychological Association (n.d.). Contempt. In *APA dictionary of psychology*. Retrieved January 18, 2023, from https://dictionary.apa.org/contempt

7. Doctor Ramani. (2022, June 3). *Are you the narcissist's storage container?* [Video]. YouTube. https://www.youtube.com/watch?v=e0XZiqRrR4Q

8. Golden, B. (2022, September 11). *Why the silent treatment is such a destructive form of passive-aggression*. Psychology Today. https://www.psychologytoday.com/us/blog/overcoming-destructive-anger/202209/why-the-silent-treatment-is-such-destructive-form-passive

9. American Psychological Association (n.d.). Behavior modification. In *APA dictionary of psychology*. Retrieved January 22, 2023, from https://dictionary.apa.org/behavior-modification

10. Kross, E., Berman, M. G., Mischel, W., Smith, E. E., & Wager, T. D. (2011). Social rejection shares somatosensory representations with physical pain. *Proceedings of the National Academy of Sciences - PNAS, 108*(15), 6270-6275. https://doi.org/10.1073/pnas.1102693108

11. Green, A., MacLean, R., & Charles, K. (2020). Unmasking gender differences in narcissism within intimate partner violence. *Personality and Individual Differences, 167*. https://doi.org/10.1016/j.paid.2020.110247

Chapter Seven

1. American Psychological Association (n.d.). Cognitive dissonance. In *APA dictionary of psychology*. Retrieved January 30, 2023, from https://dictionary.apa.org/cognitive-dissonance

2. Day, N. J. S., Townsend, M. L., & Grenyer, B. F. S. (2022). Pathological narcissism: An analysis of interpersonal dysfunction within intimate relationships. *Personality and Mental Health, 16*(3), 204-216. https://doi.org/10.1002/pmh.1532

3. American Psychological Association (n.d.). Self-fulfilling prophecy. In *APA dictionary of psychology*. Retrieved January 30, 2023, from https://dictionary.apa.org/self-fulfilling-prophecy

4. Clarke, J. (2019, August 5). *Polyvagal theory and how it relates to social cues.* Verywell Mind. https://www.verywellmind.com/polyvagal-theory-4588049

5. American Psychological Association (n.d.). Perception. In *APA dictionary of psychology*. Retrieved January 30, 2023, from https://dictionary.apa.org/perception

6. American Psychological Association (n.d.). Sympathetic nervous system. In *APA dictionary of psychology*. Retrieved January 30, 2023, from https://dictionary.apa.org/sympathetic-nervous-system

7. Thau, L., Gandhi, J., & Sharma, S. (2022, August 29). Physiology, cortisol. StatPearls [Internet]. https://www.ncbi.nlm.nih.gov/books/NBK538239/

8. American Psychological Association (n.d.). Stimulus generalization. In *APA dictionary of psychology*. Retrieved January 30, 2023, from https://dictionary.apa.org/stimulus-generalization

9. Mayo Clinic Staff. (2021, July 8). *Stress management.* https://www.mayoclinic.org/healthy-lifestyle/stress-management/in-depth/stress/art-20046037

10. WebMD Editorial Contributors. (2021, October 25). *What is hypervigilance?* https://www.webmd.com/mental-health/what-is-hypervigilance

11. Hanazawa H. (2022). Polyvagal theory and its clinical potential: An overview. *Brain and Nerve 74*(8), 1011–1016. https://doi.org/10.11477/mf.1416202169

12. Khiron Clinics. (2021, January 8). *The subtle effects of trauma: People pleasing.* https://khironclinics.com/blog/people-pleasing/

Chapter Eight

1. Resnick, A. (2022, November 23). *What is trauma bonding?* Verywell Mind. https://www.verywellmind.com/trauma-bonding-5207136

2. Fallon, H. (2014). *Social connectedness as a biological imperative: A polyvagal perspective (an interview with Stephen Porges).* American Group Psychotherapy Association and International Board for Certification of Group Psychotherapists. https://agpa.org/docs/default-source/practice-resources--group-circle/2014_winter_group_circle.pdf?sfvrsn=2e0a95a9_2

3. Brittanica. (n.d.). Attachment theory. In *Brittanica.com dictionary.* Retrieved February 2, 2023, from https://www.britannica.com/science/attachment-theory

4. American Psychological Association (n.d.). Intermittent reinforcement. In *APA dictionary of psychology.* Retrieved January 30, 2023, from https://dictionary.apa.org/intermittent-reinforcement

5. Bromberg-Martin, E. S., Matsumoto, M., & Hikosaka, O. (2010). Dopamine in motivational control: Rewarding, aversive, and alerting. *Neuron, 68*(5), 815–834. https://doi.org/10.1016/j.neuron.2010.11.022

6. Doctor Ramani. (2019, December 2). *Euphoric recall keeps you trapped in the narcissist's web.* [Video]. YouTube. https://www.youtube.com/watch?v=06QEn0oTkMQ

Chapter Nine

1. American Psychological Association (n.d.). Mirroring. In *APA dictionary of psychology.* Retrieved January 30, 2023, from https://dictionary.apa.org/mirroring

2. American Psychological Association (n.d.). Metacognition. In *APA dictionary of psychology.* Retrieved January 30, 2023, from https://dictionary.apa.org/metacognition

3. American Psychological Association (n.d.). Mindfulness. In *APA dictionary of psychology.* Retrieved January 30, 2023, from https://dictionary.apa.org/mindfulness

4. Tarbox, J., Szabo, T. G., & Aclan, M. (2020). Acceptance and commitment training within the scope of practice of applied behavior analysis. *Behavior Analysis in Practice, 15*(1), 11–32. https://doi.org/10.1007/s40617-020-00466-3

5. American Psychological Association (n.d.). Distress tolerance. In *APA dictionary of psychology*. Retrieved January 30, 2023, from https://dictionary.apa.org/distress-tolerance

6. IFS Institute. (2023). *The internal family systems model outline.* https://ifs-institute.com/resources/articles/internal-family-systems-model-outline

7. Neff, K. (2023). *Self-compassion: The three elements of self-compassion..* Self-compassion. https://self-compassion.org/the-three-elements-of-self-compassion-2/

8. Lilius, J., Kanov, J., Dutton, J., Worline, M., & Maitlis, S. (2011). *Compassion revealed: What we know about compassion at work (and where we need to know more).* Oxford University Press.

9. Just Mind. (2012, December 3). *What to do when you are having a panic attack.* https://justmind.org/what-to-do-when-you-are-having-a-panic-attack/

10. Psychological and Counseling Services Staff. (2023). *What is grounding.* University of New Hampshire. https://www.unh.edu/pacs/what-grounding

Chapter Ten

1. Holland, M. (2022, June 8). *Dysfunctional family: Signs, causes, and how to cope.* Choosing Therapy. https://www.choosingtherapy.com/dysfunctional-family/

2. Lewis, R. (2021, September 23). *What is parentification?* Healthline. https://www.healthline.com/health/parentification

3. American Psychological Association (n.d.). Temperament. In *APA dictionary of psychology*. Retrieved February 5, 2023, from https://dictionary.apa.org/temperament

4. Orloff, J. (2019). *The difference between empaths and highly sensitive people.* https://drjudithorloff.com/the-difference-between-empaths-and-highly-sensitive-people/

5. Orloff, J. (2019). *Are you an empath? 20 question self-assessment test.* https://drjudithorloff.com/quizzes/are-you-an-empath-20-question-self-assessment-test/

6. Pignatiello, G. A., Martin, R. J., & Hickman, R. L., Jr. (2020). Decision fatigue: A conceptual analysis. *Journal of Health Psychology, 25*(1), 123–135. https://doi.org/10.1177/1359105318763510

7. Pluut, H., & Wonders, J. (2020). Not able to lead a healthy life when you need it the most: Dual role of lifestyle behaviors in the association of blurred

work-life boundaries with well-being. *Frontiers in Psychology, 11.*
https://doi.org/10.3389/fpsyg.2020.607294

8. WebMD Editorial Contributors. (2021, October 25). *Setting boundaries.*
https://www.webmd.com/mental-health/setting-boundaries

9. Ishler, J. (2021, August 12). *Sleep tips for the highly sensitive person.*
Healthline. https://www.healthline.com/health/sleep/sleep-tips-for-the-highly-sensitive-person

Chapter Eleven

1. Quoidbach, J., Gilbert, D. T., & Wilson, T. D. (2013). The end of history illusion. *American Association for the Advancement of Science, 339*(6115), 96-98. https://doi.org/10.1126/science.1229294

2. WebMD Editorial Contributors. (2022, November 19). *Men and anger management.* https://www.webmd.com/men/guide/anger-management

Chapter Twelve

1. Cote, C. (2022, March 10). *Growth mindset vs. fixed mindset: What's the difference?* Harvard Business School Online.
https://online.hbs.edu/blog/post/growth-mindset-vs-fixed-mindset

2. Cote, C. (2022, March 10). *Growth mindset vs. fixed mindset: What's the difference?* Harvard Business School Online.
https://online.hbs.edu/blog/post/growth-mindset-vs-fixed-mindset

Chapter Thirteen

1. Tedeschi, R. (2020, August). *Growth after trauma.* Harvard Business Review. https://hbr.org/2020/07/growth-after-trauma

2. Arabi, S. (2022). *PTSD Symptoms: Romantic relationships with individuals who have narcissistic and psychopathic traits.* [Master's thesis, Harvard University Division of Continuing Education]. ProQuest Dissertations Publishing. https://dash.harvard.edu/handle/1/37371611

3. Collier, L. (2016, November). *Growth after trauma: Why are some people more resilient than others—and can it be taught?* American Psychological Association. https://www.apa.org/monitor/2016/11/growth-trauma

4. Tedeschi, R. G., & Calhoun, L. G. (1996). The posttraumatic growth inventory: Measuring the positive legacy of trauma. *Journal of Traumatic Stress, 9*(3), 455–471. https://doi.org/10.1007/BF02103658

5. Bartlett, C. (2008). *Kintsugi—Art of repair.* Traditional Kyoto. https://traditionalkyoto.com/culture/kintsugi/

6. Scott, E. (2022, September 12). *What is pessimism?* Verywell Mind. https://www.verywellmind.com/is-it-safer-to-be-a-pessimist-3144874

7. Shaw, A., Joseph, S., & Linley, P. A. (2005). Religion, spirituality, and posttraumatic growth: A systematic review. *Mental Health, Religion & Culture, 8*(1), 1-11. https://doi.org/10.1080/1367467032000157981

INDEX

C

D

H

I